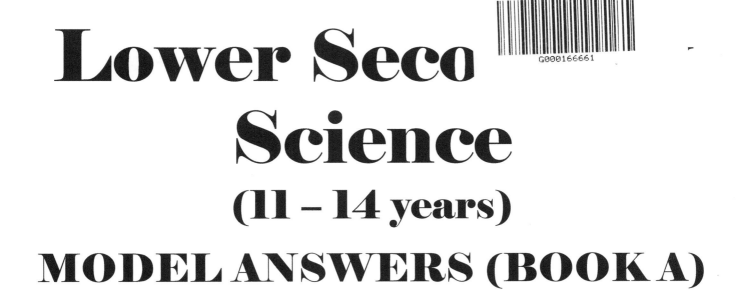

Lower Seco Science
(11 – 14 years)
MODEL ANSWERS (BOOK A)

Chris Prescott

MAPLE
PUBLISHERS

Lower Secondary Science (11 – 14 years)

Author: Chris Prescott

Copyright © Chris Prescott (2022)

The right of Chris Prescott to be identified as author of this work has been asserted by the author in accordance with section 77 and 78 of the Copyright, Designs and Patents Act 1988.

First Published in 2022

ISBN 978-1-915164-64-3 (Paperback)

Cover Design, Illustrations and Book Layout by:
White Magic Studios
www.whitemagicstudios.co.uk

Published by:
Maple Publishers
1 Brunel Way,
Slough,
SL1 1FQ, UK
www.maplepublishers.com

A CIP catalogue record for this title is available from the British Library.

CONTENTS

Introduction

The aim of this book is to identify and encourage model answers in order to achieve top grades in science.

Each topic of the book is divided into sections to match the content of the Lower Secondary Science Syllabus.

Each section is divided into three steps.

Step I Key Knowledge.

Identifies key knowledge for the section. Any common errors and misconceptions are also identified.

Step II Be the Teacher

Tests your understanding of what is being looked for in a particular question by asking you to mark and grade three model answers to the question. One of the answers is a Grade A answer, another a Grade C answer. The third answer is a wildcard and could be any grade. Examiner's comments then follow to explain the correct mark and grade for the model answers.

Step III Test Yourself

Questions to test your understanding of the particular section of a topic. Includes a mark scheme which identifies the various possible responses to more open ended questions.

Ten Hints Toward Model Answers

1. **Always read all of the question** very thoroughly so the answers you give are relevant to the question.

2. **There is no need to include the question** in your answer. No marks are awarded for telling the examiner what he has already told you.

3. With free response questions it is sometimes worth spending a few minutes **planning your answer** so all the points are covered in a neat and organised way.

4. **Do not spend more than the allocated time** on a particular question. In most questions the best quality of an answer normally comes at the beginning. If a question is worth 4 marks then scoring the first two marks in your answer is usually much easier than scoring the last two marks.

5. **Look to see how many marks the question is worth**. For each mark there is a marking point the examiner is looking for. If the question is worth four marks you need to make four points in your answer to score full marks.

6. **Do not use abbreviations in your answer**. They may be meaningful to you but not to the examiner.

7. **Always show working in questions that involve calculations**. You are only penalised for an incorrect stage in a calculation so you can score marks even though you end up with the wrong answer.

8. **In most calculation questions you should include units** in your answer.

   There is often one mark allocated for giving the correct unit in a calculation.

9. **Do not give ambiguous answers.** No marks are given for describing the change in colour of litmus paper as 'reddish-blue'. Giving a list of possible answers is asking the examiner to choose for you, so will not score marks.

   (Unless all of your list is completely correct).

10. **Always follow instructions** and do not try to be 'too clever'. Giving a chemical formula when asked for a chemical name does not score any marks.

ANSWERING DIFFERENT TYPES OF QUESTIONS

Multiple Choice

Multiple choice type questions are popular in science as they can be marked objectively and quickly. Also they do not penalise a candidate whose writing ability is weak.

Most multiple choice questions consist of a statement or question which is called the 'stem'. This is then followed by four different alternatives (A, B, C and D), only one of which is correct. The three wrong answers are called 'distractors'.

1. The *distractors are sometimes only partly correct*, so it is important to read carefully all four possible alternatives even though the correct answer looks obvious.

2. If you cannot decide between several alternative answers always make an intelligent guess. *Do not leave a multiple choice question blank.*

3. *There are never two multiple choice answers that are both correct.* If you tick two answers as being correct you will automatically not score any marks, even though one of the answers was correct.

4. *Do not look for patterns or sequences in your answers.* They do not exist. There is no equal distribution of As, Bs. etc. and do not be concerned if you last three answers were all C!

Structured Questions

Most structured questions, as their name implies, are broken down into sections. After each section is a space left for the answer.

1. The *size of the space that is left indicates the extent of the expected response*.

2. *The mark* usually given in brackets after the question *indicates the number of marking points*.

3. *If a question is only worth one mark* then you only need to say one thing to answer the question. *Do not waste time giving lots of detail*.

4. *Writing must be legible.* If the answer can't be read no mark can be awarded. Accurate spelling is not essential as long as the word sounds like the correct answer.

Free-Response Questions

These type of questions can be 'open-ended' and are often the most difficult to score good marks on.

1. *Make sure you read the whole of the question* before you start your answer.

2. *Perhaps draw up a plan of your answer before-hand* so you can break your answer into stages.

3. *It is quality and not quantity of the answer that is important.* The best quality usually comes at the beginning of the answer, so do not waste too much time trying to achieve full marks in a free-response question.

4. *In most questions any information given in the question stem should be used somewhere in your answer.* If you have not used this information then think again about your answer.

5. *In calculations if you have used a calculator check that the size of your answer is about right.* Try rounding the numbers up and working out a rough answer in your head to check the size of your answer.

Multiple Choice Question	Hints for Model Answer
When water evaporates from a puddle and changes into water vapour its _____ A density remains the same but its volume increases B. density decreases as its volume increases C. density decreases as its volume decreases D. density and volume remain the same	**Answer B Remember the following points** • **Read all four alternatives before you decide on an answer.** • **Read all of the answer as answer C also starts off correct.** • **Eliminate those answers that are obviously incorrect. For example C and D as volume must increase when change to gas.** • **Only one answer is totally correct**

Structured Question	Hints for Model Answer
Copper metal, which is much cheaper than gold, is often mixed with gold when making rings. The amount of gold present in the mixture is indicated by the number of carats.	(a) In a calculation you must show working eg

Copper metal, which is much cheaper than gold, is often mixed with gold when making rings. The amount of gold present in the mixture is indicated by the number of carats.

A 24-carat gold ring is pure gold with no copper. [Density of gold = 19.3 g/cm^3

Density of copper = 8.9 g/cm^3]

Consider these two rings:

Ring A   Ring B

9-carat gold   18-carat gold

mass = 36.0 g   mass = 25.3 g

volume = 3.3 cm^3 volume = 2.0 cm^3

(a) Calculate the density of ring A.

....

.... [3 marks]

(b) Calculate the density of ring B.

....

.... [3 marks]

(c) Identify the ring that contains the highest percentage of copper.

.... [1 mark]

(d) Suggest the density of a 24 carat ring.

....

.... [2 marks]

Hints for Model Answer

(a) In a calculation you must show working eg

$$\text{Density} = \frac{\text{mass}}{\text{volume}} = \frac{36.0}{3.3}$$ [1 mark]

$$= 10.91$$ [1 mark]

$$\text{g/cm}^3$$ [1 mark]

In most calculations a mark is allocated for correct units.

(b) Same marking scheme as in (a)

$$\text{Density} = \frac{\text{mass}}{\text{volume}} = \frac{25.3}{2.0}$$ [1 mark]

$$= 12.65$$ [1 mark]

$$\text{g/cm}^3$$ [1 mark]

(c) As there is only one mark allocated for the question there is only one correct point to make. This is also indicated by only one line for the answer and the command word 'name' instead of 'explain'.

9-carat ring [1 mark]

[Unnecessary to explain your choice in terms of copper has lowest density so 9–carat ring has most copper.]

(d) Two marks so two points to make. This is indicated by two lines for answer and command word 'suggest'.

Density of ring is 19. 3 g/cm^3 [1 mark]

This is because 24–carat indicates pure gold. [1 mark]

	Free Response Question						Hints for Model Answer

Free Response Question

The table shows how the mass of a liquid changes as its volume changes

mass (g)	15	25	45	60	70	100
volume (cm³)	30	50	90	120	140	200

Plot a graph of these results and use the graph to calculate the density of the liquid.

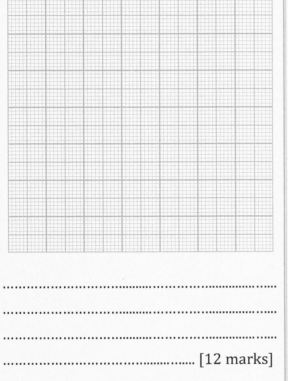

....

....

....

.... [12 marks]

Hints for Model Answer

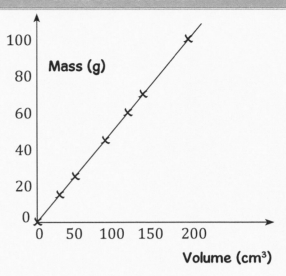

Marks for graph as follows:

1. Suitable scale on x-axis to cover graph paper [1 mark]

2. Suitable scale on y-axis to cover graph paper [1 mark]

3. Label both axes with correct units [1 mark]

4. Correct plotting of points. [3 marks]

5. Plotting graph through origin. [1 mark]

6. Correct line of best fit through points [1 mark]

Slope/gradient of graph is [1 mark]

$= \dfrac{mass}{volume}$

$= density$ [1 mark]

$= \dfrac{100}{200} = 0.5$ [1 mark]

$= 0.5$ g/cm³ [1 mark]

Command Words

Command words are the words that are used in questions to direct you to the answer the examiner is looking for. It is important that the student understands the meaning of the command word so they give the correct answer.

Calculate (or **Determine)** Give a numerical answer based on a formula.

Classify	To group things based on common characteristics.
Compare	Identify similarities and differences.
Complete	Add words, numbers, labels or plots to complete a sentence, table, diagram or graph.
Deduce	Draw a conclusion based on general rules.
Describe	Set out the facts or characteristics in a particular situation or experiment.
Distinguish	To identify and understand differences.
Draw (or Construct)	Produce a diagram/drawing with sufficient detail and labels.
Estimate	Suggest an approximate value with appropriate units.
Evaluate	To consider all factors then give an appropriate judgement or conclusion.
Explain	Requires a short answer (length indicated by number of lines for answer) with some supporting argument.
Identify (or **Name**)	To select and/or name an object, event, concept or process.
Infer	Draw a conclusion based on observations.
Investigate	To find out by carrying out experiments.
Label	Classify or add identifying words to diagram.
List	State a number of points or items without elaboration.
Measure	Determine a numeric value.
Outline	To give the main essential points.
Plot	Translate data into suitable graph or chart with labelled axes.
Predict	Write down possible outcomes.
Recognise	To identify facts, characteristics or concepts that are needed to understand a situation.
Show	Write down details, steps or calculations to prove an answer.
Sketch	Provide a simple freehand drawing.
Suggest	Apply scientific knowledge from the syllabus to a new related situation.
State (or **Write down)**	Provide a concise answer with no supporting argument.

Common Errors

- You cannot see a colourless gas……….only bubbles or fizzing
- You cannot see heat……..only a temperature rise
- Clear is not colourless…….you can have a clear blue solution
- You cannot lose heat…….only transfer heat
- You cannot lose mass……only transfer mass
- You cannot see a force…….only its effect

Drawing Diagrams

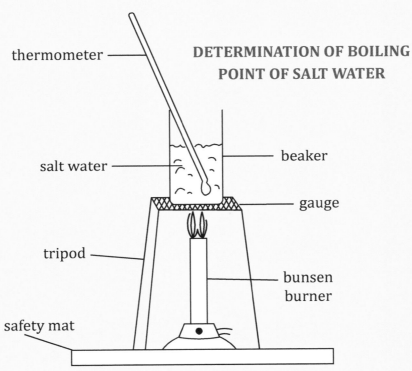

DETERMINATION OF BOILING POINT OF SALT WATER

thermometer — salt water — beaker — gauge — tripod — bunsen burner — safety mat

Things to remember to do:

- Give the diagram a title
- Draw diagram in pencil so can change and rub-out if necessary
- Each part of the diagram should be fully labelled
- The diagram should be large enough to see important details
- The size of different parts of diagram should be in proportion

Drawing Graphs

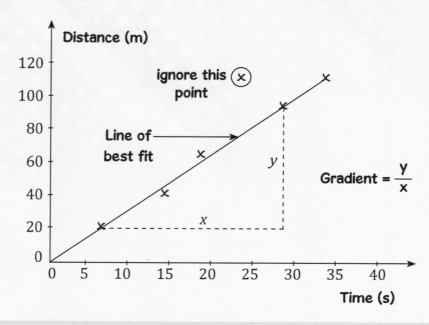

Things to remember to do:

- Choose suitable scales so the graph takes up most of the available graph paper

- Don't choose a scale which leaves the small squares equal to a number which is difficult to divide up

- Label both the axes with units

- Plot points with a fine pencil

- Draw a line of best fit. It does not have to go through all the points. Omit the points (outlier point) which obviously do not fit the pattern.

- The line of best fit does not have to go through the origin.

- To find a value on the y-axis which corresponds with an x-axis value, draw a vertical line from the x-value to the line of best fit. Then draw a horizontal line from where the vertical line touches the line of best fit, to the y-axis

- Gradient (slope) of the graph is found by the amount it changes on the y-axis divided by the amount it changes on the x-axis.

Scientific Endeavour

A. Scientific Studies

Step I Key Knowledge

- **Science** is the **systematic study of the natural and physical world** through observation, experimentation and analysis.

- Science is not confined to the laboratory and shows itself in **all aspects of our lives**.

- Three main areas of science are **Physics**, **Chemistry** and **Biology**.

Science

Physics is the study of matter and energy including light, sound, electricity, magnetism, radiation (heat) and motion.	**Chemistry** is the study of molecular structures of matter and their interactions.	**Biology** is the study of living things from the tiniest microscopic organisms to the largest whales.

- Science can give meaningful explanations of why things happen and help to predict what might happen in the future.

Common Errors

- Scientific knowledge never changes....it does because research improves and some scientific theories have to be modified.

- Science can solve all of society's problems....it cannot and sometimes creates problems such as pollution, global warming and drug abuse.

- Science helps to create machines and inventions which improve our surroundings and the quality of life. We call the use of scientific knowledge for practical purposes **technology**. Examples are in areas like communication (information technology), transportation, medicine and computers.

Step II Be the Teacher

Each question is followed by three model answers.

One of these answers is a Grade A answer (above 80% correct), another a Grade C answer (around 50% correct). The third answer could be any grade (A to E).

Mark all three answers giving an appropriate grade with reasoning.

Question 1

Explain the different areas of science studied in Physics, Chemistry and Biology.

[6 marks]

Answer 1

Physics is the study of moving things and energy whereas chemistry studies chemical compounds. Biology studies man and animals.

Mark [ ]   Grade [ ]

Reasoning:..

....

Answer 2

Physics is the study of things you cannot see whereas Chemistry studies things you can see. Biology is the study of living things you see.

Mark [ ]   Grade [ ]

Reasoning:..

....

Answer 3

Physics is the study of matter and energy whereas chemistry studies materials and substance. Biology studies living things like plants and animals.

Mark [ ]   Grade [ ]

Reasoning:..

....

Actual Mark and Grade for Question 1

Answer 1

Physics is the study of moving things and energy whereas chemistry studies chemical compounds. Biology studies man and animals.

Mark	3		Grade	C

Reasoning: Only one mark for Physics as moving things have kinetic energy so same marking point for 'study of energy'. Physics also studies matter (second marking point). A fully correct answer which scores both marks must not have any exceptions or omissions. [1]

Only one mark out of two for Chemistry as does include the study of chemical compounds but also other materials which are not compounds, like mixtures or elements (metals and non-metals). [1]

Only one mark for biology as does include the study of man and animals but also other living things like plants and bacteria. [1]

Answer 2

Physics is the study of things you cannot see whereas Chemistry studies things you can see. Biology is the study of living things you see.

Mark	2		Grade	D

Reasoning: Biology scored both marks for an accurate definition as 'the study of living things'. It also studies things you can't see, like bacteria, but it would be harsh to penalise. [2]

No marks were scored for Physics or Chemistry. You can see the effects in Physics of forces and matter. You cannot see atoms of elements, which are studied in Chemistry. [0]

Answer 3

Physics is the study of matter and energy whereas chemistry studies materials and substance. Biology studies living things like plants and animals.

Mark	6		Grade	A

Reasoning: All three sciences scored both marks. Each definition was accurate with no exceptions [6]

Question 2

A recent scientific invention has been the smart phone. State advantages and possible disadvantages of such a device. [5 marks]

Answer 1

With smart phones you can download games, take pictures and go online to find out information about all sorts of different things. However smartphones can be used for bullying and some websites are very rude.

Mark [ ]   Grade [ ]

Reasoning:..

....

Answer 2

Smart phones are easy to carry around but can fall out your pocket and smash. Also they are expensive to repair but look great when new.

Having a smart phone helps you to make friends and be popular.

Mark [ ]   Grade [ ]

Reasoning:..

....

Answer 3

Advantages - attractive and can take pictures. You can send messages and phone friends.

Disadvantages - expensive and can pester somebody by phoning them all the time

Mark [ ]   Grade [ ]

Reasoning:..

....

Actual Mark and Grade for Question 2

Answer 1

With smart phones you can download games take pictures and go online to find out information about different things. However smartphones can be used for bullying and some websites are very rude.

| Mark | 5 | | Grade | A |

Reasoning: As 5 marks are allocated for this question we are looking for 3 advantages and 2 disadvantages.

Advantages of smart phone: need three distinct advantages

allow: portable or fits in pocket/ contact friends or send messages/ connect to internet or social media or websites or download apps/ camera or take pictures/ play games or different apps/ use to find out answers to all sorts of questions or source of knowledge (other possible acceptable advantages)

ignore: attractive / light / strong / any personal judgements   [3]

Disadvantages of smart phone: need two distinct disadvantages

allow: often distracted by incoming mail or texts/ possible access to unpleasant website material / can be used for bullying (other possible acceptable disadvantages)

ignore: expensive /easy to break / easy to misplace/ any personal judgements [2]

Answer 2

Smart phones are easy to carry around but can fall out your pocket and smash. Also they are expensive to repair but look great when new.

Having a smart phone helps you to make friends and be popular.

| Mark | 0 | | Grade | E |

Reasoning: The advantages and disadvantages are mixed up together. There are no marks scored as the comments are personal conclusions and therefore unacceptable answers. A smart phone can keep you in contact with friends but does not necessarily help you to make friends.   [0]

Answer 3

Advantages – attractive and can take ✓ pictures. You can send ✓ messages and phone friends.

Disadvantages – expensive and can pester ✓ somebody by phoning them all the time.

Mark	3		Grade	C

Reasoning: In this question it is a good idea to clearly split one's answer into advantages and disadvantages.

They need to be distinct answers. For example send message and phone friends scores only one mark. With advantages 'attractive' is too vague and personal to score. However two marks for advantages are scored as taking pictures and sending messages each score one mark. [2]

With disadvantages only one mark out of two is scored. Expensive is too vague and relative. However 'pestering somebody by phoning' is the equivalent of bullying. [1]

Step III Test Yourself

1. State what we call the use of scientific knowledge for practical purposes?

    .... [1]

2. Science has helped to produce different fuels. Identify two pollution problems resulting from such fuels.

    .... [2]

3. Which of these scientific inventions has a beneficial outcome on society?

    1. New materials   2. New social drugs   3. Smaller computer chips

    A. 1 and 2   B. 1 and 3   C. 2 and 3   D. 1, 2 and 3   [ ]   [1]

4. Identify which of these statements about knowledge obtained through science is/are true?

(a) Scientific knowledge is subject to change.   ....   [1]

(b) Scientific knowledge can be harmful.   ....   [1]

(c) Scientific knowledge increases every day.   ....   [1]

(d) Scientific knowledge can prolong life.   ....   [1]

5. Complete this table by ticking the science associated with the area of study.

Area of study	Biology	Chemistry	Physics
Types of fungus			
Reactivity of metals			
Speed of light			
Strength of magnet			
Pull of gravity			
Size of atom			
Types of disease			
Weight of object			

[8]

6. A recent scientific invention has been the electric car. Identify advantages and possible disadvantages of these cars.

....

....

....

....

[4]

MODEL ANSWERS

1. technology [1]

   allow: applied science

2. **allow**: acid rain /greenhouse gases or global warming/ smoke particles or soot

   ignore: named pollutant like carbon dioxide or sulfur dioxide or carbon / vague answers like 'smells' or 'poisonous gases' [2]

3. B [1]

4. (a) true [1]   (b) true [1]   (c) true [1]   (d) true [1]

5.

Area of study	Biology	Chemistry	Physics
Types of fungus	✓		
Reactivity of metals		✓	
Speed of light			✓
Strength of magnet			✓
Pull of gravity			✓
Size of atom		✓	
Types of disease	✓		
Weight of object			✓

[8]

6. Advantages of electric car: need two distinct advantages
   allow: quieter or less noisy / less pollution or any named pollutant from fossil fuels / helps conserve crude oil or saves non-renewable resource /
   (other possible acceptable advantages)
   ignore: attractive / reliable / faster / any personal judgements   [2]

   Disadvantages of electric car: need two distinct disadvantages
   allow: not travel as far without charging as a fuel engine / fewer stations (than petrol) to recharge battery / perhaps more accidents as cannot hear cars coming
   (other possible acceptable disadvantages)
   ignore: expensive / goes slower / less reliable / any personal judgements   [2]

   Total 20 marks

B. Safety Rules in the Science laboratory

Step I Key Knowledge

- A **science laboratory** should be a safe place for conducting experiments. To ensure that it is **safe to work** in, the following safety rules should be observed.

	Safety Rules
1	Do not enter a laboratory or carry out any experiments without supervision from your teacher.

	Safety Rules
2	Do not run around in a laboratory. Leave coats and schoolbags outside the laboratory.
3	Do not eat or drink in the laboratory.
4	Read all instructions carefully before carrying out any experiment.
5	Handle all equipment and materials carefully. Never touch or taste chemicals.
6	Always wear safety goggles when heating or mixing chemicals.
7	Report all accidents, breakages or spillages immediately.
8	Try to keep your workbench clean and dry. Dispose of all chemicals in waste bins, not down the sink.
9	Never remove any chemicals or apparatus from the laboratory.
10	Remember when in doubt whether something is safe or not to ask your teacher.

- Many chemicals used in the laboratory can be dangerous. These substances have hazard symbols on the labels of their containers. The important **hazard symbols** are:

Hazard	Symbol
Explosive Substance may react violently when heated or struck. It must be handled carefully. **Example:** Flash powder	
Flammable Substance catches fire easily. It must be kept away from naked flames. **Examples:** Petrol, alcohol, kerosene, hydrogen	
Acute toxicity Substance causes harmful effects on the body when breathed in, swallowed or upon contact with the skin. Always wash your hands after handling it. **Example:** Carbon monoxide, cyanide, mercury, chlorine	

Hazard	Symbol
Harmful or irritant Substance which causes irritation to the eyes, respiratory system, and/or skin. When handling it, always use a spatula. **Examples:** Phenol, chloroform	
Corrosive Substance may cause severe damage to body parts. You must quickly wash with tap water if such substance is spilled. **Examples:** Sulphuric acid, nitric acid, sodium hydroxide solution	
Environmental toxicity Substance which is harmful to the environment **Examples:** ammonia, mercury, zinc oxide	

Common Errors

- Inflammable substances do not catch alight easily……they do and should be kept well away from naked flames. It is best to describe such substances as flammable. Look out for the flammable Hazard Symbol.

Step II Be the Teacher

This question is followed by three model answers.

One of these answers is a Grade A answer (above 80% correct), another a Grade C answer (around 50% correct). The third answer could be any grade (A to E).

Mark all three answers giving an appropriate grade with reasoning.

Question

Explain why it is unwise to take coats and school bags into the science laboratory?

[3 marks]

Answer 1

It is unwise to take bags and coats into the science laboratory as they will get mixed up so you won't be able to find your books or writing equipment.

Mark [ ]   Grade [ ]

Reasoning: ....

....

Answer 2

Students may trip over bags or coats on the floor. It is very dangerous to fall over when carrying chemicals or glass equipment. The chemicals may be corrosive or poisonous and the glass will smash and cut the skin

Mark		Grade	

Reasoning: ....
....
....
....
....

Answer 3

Students may not see the bags on the floor and might trip over them.

Mark		Grade	

Reasoning: ....
....
....
....

Actual Mark and Grade for Question

Answer 1

It is unwise to take bags and coats into the science laboratory as they will get mixed up so you won't be able to find your books or writing equipment.

Mark	0	Grade	E

Reasoning: The student has copied out the question and there is no attempt by the student to bring in any safety implications of having bags and coats on the floor of the laboratory, so no marks can be scored.

Answer 2

Students may trip over bags or coats on the floor. It is very dangerous to fall over when carrying chemicals or glass equipment. The chemicals may be corrosive or poisonous and the glass will smash and cut the skin.

Mark	3		Grade	A

Reasoning: Possible safety implications were fully explored by the student. The tripping and falling over was then followed through by with the scientific hazards of chemicals and broken glass equipment.

Answer 3

Students may not see the bags and might trip over them.

Mark	1		Grade	D

Reasoning: Although the student pointed out the hazard of tripping over, they did not expand and explain what could happen if the student was carrying equipment or chemicals. Also there is the possibility of falling and knocking over laboratory apparatus set out on the work benches.

Step III Test Yourself

1. Match the hazard symbol to its correct identity by drawing a line to connect them.

 •   • Corrosive

 •   • Explosive

 •   • Flammable

 •   • Acute toxicity

 •   • Harmful or irritant

 •   • Environmental toxicity

[6]

2. In this list of chemicals one of them has a different safety hazard from the other two. Identify which one and explain your choice.

(a) nitric acid   alcohol   sodium hydroxide solution

....
....
.... [2]

(b) mercury   petrol   kerosine

....
....
.... [2]

(c) alcohol   flash powder   kerosine

....
....
.... [2]

(d) sulfuric acid   potassium hydroxide solution   chloroform

....
....
.... [2]

3. When heating a solid in a test tube in the school laboratory identify **three** safety precautions you would observe, explaining how they make the experiment more safe.

(i) ....
....
.... [2]

(ii) ....
....
.... [2]

(iii)..
....
.... [2]

MODEL ANSWERS

1. Flammable sign   Corrosive   [1]

    Harmful or irritant sign   Explosive   [1]

    Environmental toxicity sign   Flammable   [1]

    Acute toxicity sign   Acute toxicity   [1]

    Corrosive sign   Harmful or irritant   [1]

    Explosive sign   Environmental toxicity   [1]

2. (a) Alcohol is flammable [1] but nitric acid and sodium hydroxide
    are both corrosive. [1]

    allow: alcohol flammable other two corrosive [2]

            alcohol inflammable but others not [1]

    ignore: alcohol different from other two

    (b) Mercury is acutely toxic [1] but petrol and kerosene are both flammable. [1]

    allow: mercury is environmentally toxic [1]

    (c) Flash powder is explosive [1] but alcohol and kerosene are both flammable.
    [1]

    (d) Chloroform is harmful or irritant [1] but sulfuric acid and potassium
    hydroxide are both corrosive. [1]

3. (i)   Hold the test tube with tongs [1] to avoid burning your hand   [1]

          ignore: not hold with hands

    (ii)   Point the test tube away from yourself and others [1] so that if anything
    erupts out of the test tube it will not harm anybody.   [1]

          ignore: point upwards

          allow: don't look into the test tube [1], wear eye protection   [1]

(iii) Only put a small amount of the solid into the test tube. [1] There is less chance of the solid reaching the top of the tube and escaping. [1]

ignore: don't handle solid, use a spatula to measure solid

allow: only quarter fill test tube [1], heat gently [1], use small flame [1]

stop heating if powder rises up [1]

Total 20 marks

C. Common Laboratory Equipment

Step I Key Knowledge

- There are many types of **laboratory equipment** and **apparatus**, especially glassware, in your school laboratory. You should know how to use simple apparatus and be able to draw **sectional diagrams** of such apparatus. The diagrams are in outline but must be in the correct proportions.

Common Errors

- It is thought that measurements collected by a data logger are more accurate than data collected by people.

  This in untrue. The data collected is not more accurate but can be collected at regular time intervals, over prolonged periods of time and under inhospitable conditions.

- The **Bunsen burner** is used for heating substances in a school laboratory. Always before you light the Bunsen burner make sure the air-hole is closed.

- There are two types of Bunsen flame, depending on whether the air-hole is open or closed. The **luminous flame** is obtained when the air-hole is closed and the **non-luminous flame** is obtained when the air-hole is open.

Luminous flame	Non-luminous flame
- **Visible** with a whitish-yellow zone caused by the incomplete burning of the gas.	- Pale blue and **difficult to see**. When not using the Bunsen flame, switch to a luminous flame as it is easier to see, and therefore safer.

Luminous flame	Non-luminous flame
• **Smoky** because particles of carbon formed during the incomplete combustion. • Unsteady and **not very hot**.	• **Clean** as there is sufficient air entering the barrel to allow all of the gas to burn completely. • Steady, strong and **very hot**

Common Errors

- It is often thought the hottest part of a Bunsen flame is inside the flame, just above the Bunsen chimney.

- This is not true as there is a cone of unburnt gas just above the chimney. The hottest part of the flame is just above this cone of unburnt gas.

Step II Be the Teacher

The question is followed by three model answers.

One of these answers is a Grade A answer (above 80% correct), another a Grade C answer (around 50% correct). The third answer could be any grade (A to E).

Mark all three answers giving an appropriate grade with reasoning.

Question

Describe the procedure for safely lighting-up a Bunsen burner in the laboratory.

[4 marks]

Answer 1

1. Place the Bunsen burner on a safety mat.
2. Close the air-hole of the Bunsen burner.
3. Light up a splint and hold it above the Bunsen chimney.
4. Turn on the gas tap and light the flame.
5. Extinguish the splint. Make sure it is not glowing.

Mark		Grade	

Reasoning: ....

....

....

Answer 2

Switch on the gas and light the Bunsen burner with a match that is held over the chimney.

Mark [ ]   **Grade** [ ]

Reasoning:..
....
....
....
....

Answer 3

Make sure the air-hole of the Bunsen burner is closed. Light the burner with a lighted splint above the chimney, making sure you remove your hand as quickly as possible.

Mark [ ]   **Grade** [ ]

Reasoning:..
....
....
....
....

Actual Mark and Grade for Question

Answer 1

1. Place the Bunsen burner on a safety mat. ✓
2. Close the air-hole of the Bunsen burner. ✓
3. Light up a splint and hold it above the Bunsen chimney. ✓
4. Turn on the gas tap and light the flame. ✓
5. Extinguish the splint. Make sure it is not glowing.

Mark	4		Grade	A

Reasoning: The description includes over four marking points. Full marks as the student safely lit the Bunsen burner with safety precautions followed before and after lighting. It is a good idea when describing a procedure to break it down into stages and number each stage.

Answer 2

Switch on the gas and light the Bunsen burner with a match that is held over the chimney.

Mark	1		Grade	E

Reasoning: There was some attempt by the student but little thought about safety. It is very important to have a lighted splint or match above the Bunsen chimney before you switch on the gas. It is very dangerous to switch on the Bunsen burner and then go and 'search for a light'. This order of lighting first before switching on the gas is not made clear.

Answer 3

Make sure the air-hole of the Bunsen burner is closed. Light the burner with a lighted splint above the chimney, making sure you remove your hand as quickly as possible.

Mark	2		Grade	C

Reasoning: As there are four marks for the question the student should try to make four points about safely lighting the Bunsen burner. He has made only two.

Scored one mark for realising the air-hole should be closed before lighting the Bunsen burner otherwise 'strike-back' may occur. This is when the Bunsen lights at the jet inside the chimney and not on top of the chimney.

Second mark is for holding the lighted splint above the chimney. However it is not made clear that he should not switch the gas on until the lighted splint is above the chimney.

Step III Test Yourself

Consider this paragraph about common laboratory apparatus

The ....*1*......... is used to measure temperature. The ....*2*.......... accurately measures the volume of liquid added to another liquid and is more accurate than using a ....*3*.......... cylinder. To separate insoluble solids from liquids we use a ....4.......... However to heat a solid strongly with a ....*5*.......... we use a ....*6*......... with a lid to avoid the solid from spitting out.

Flasks come in different shapes. The ....*7*.......... flask is used when acids and alkalis mix together. The ....*8*........ flask is used when preparing gases by mixing chemicals and no heating is required. The ....*9*............ flask is used when distilling liquids. The vapour from such liquids is cooled so that it liquefies using a ....*10*............ .

Complete the table below by identify the ten missing apparatus [10]

Then draw sectional diagrams to represent each piece of apparatus. [10]

	Name of Apparatus	Sectional Diagram		Name of Apparatus	Sectional Diagram
1	....		2	....	
3	....		4	....	
5	....		6	....	

	Name of Apparatus	Sectional Diagram		Name of Apparatus	Sectional Diagram
7	....		8	....	
9	....		10	....	

MODEL ANSWERS

	Name of Apparatus	Sectional Diagram		Name of Apparatus	Sectional Diagram
1	Thermometer [1]	[1]	2	Burette [1]	[1]
3	Measuring (Cylinder) [1]	[1]	4	Funnel [1]	[1]
5	Bunsen burner [1]	[1]	6	Crucible [1]	[1]

	Name of Apparatus	Sectional Diagram		Name of Apparatus	Sectional Diagram
7	Conical (flask) [1]	[1]	8	Flat-bottomed (flask) [1]	[1]
9	Round-bottomed (flask) [1]	[1]	10	Condenser [1]	[1]

Total 20 marks

D. Scientific Inquiry

Step I Key Knowledge

- **Scientific knowledge** is built up from the **systematic collection and analysis of evidence**. Be aware however that scientific evidence is subject to multiple interpretations.

- Recognise that **scientific evidence** is often gathered **quantitatively** using measuring instruments like balances etc. However evidence can also be gathered **qualitatively** through our senses.

- When recording quantitatively it is important to **record the data as accurately as possible**.

- Recorded data is normally presented in ways that **show trends in results**. Scientific results are often recorded in **table** or **chart** or **graph** form.

- **Science inquiry** is a way of practising science. In encouraging science inquiry, students use similar methods, attitudes and skills as scientists do when they are conducting scientific research.

- Besides having the correct attitude toward **science inquiry** you will also require the **scientific skills** of planning, observing, communicating and inferring.

- Scientists analyse problems in a step-by-step way which they call **scientific method.** The stages of scientific method are as follows:

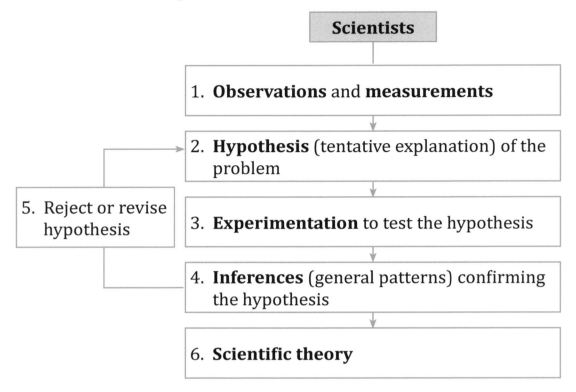

- In experimentation, the things that have an effect on the results are called **variables**.

- The **independent variable** is the variable in an experiment that you change.

- The independent variable causes the **dependent variable** to change and is the thing you measure.

- The variables that do not change in your experiment are called **controlled variables**.

- You should have as many **controlled variables** as possible to make the comparison a **fair test**. This means that the same test, under the same conditions, produces the same result each time.

Common Errors

Some people think that an inference (looking for a general pattern) and a hypothesis (tentative explanation of a problem) are the same.

They are not as a hypothesis always comes before experimentation and an inference comes after experimentation.

Step II Be the Teacher

This question is followed by three model answers.

One of these answers is a Grade A answer (above 80% correct), another a Grade C answer (around 50% correct). The third answer could be any grade (A to E).

Mark all three answers giving an appropriate grade with reasoning.

Question

Deduce the various controlled variables for an experiment set up to decide which of two substances A or B dissolves better in water. [5 marks]

Answer 1

Dissolve A in a certain volume of water. Evaporate the water and weigh the solid that was dissolved. Do exactly the same for substance B.

Mark		Grade	

Reasoning: ....

....

....

Answer 2

Measure out 50 cm³ of water in a beaker. Add solid A until no more dissolves. Filter any undissolved A. Evaporate the solution to see how much of A dissolved. Do exactly the same for substance B making sure you use the same amount of water.

Mark		Grade	

Reasoning: ....

....

....

Answer 3

Measure out same volume of water at same temperature in two beakers. Stir solid A in one beaker until no more dissolves. Filter undissolved A and evaporate solution to find how much solid A dissolved.

Do same for substance B in other beaker making sure stir the same number of times

Mark		Grade	

Reasoning: ....

....

....

....

Actual Mark and Grade for Question

Answer 1

Dissolve A in a certain volume of water. Evaporate the water and weigh the solid that was dissolved. Do exactly the same for substance B

Mark	2	Grade	D

Reasoning: You must answer the question which is about identifying the controlled variables in the experiment. Only one controlled variable was identified that of a certain volume of water. [1] Evaporating or weighing are not controlled variables, unless said 'weigh with the same balance each time' or 'evaporate for a certain period of time with same Bunsen burner'.

The second mark was given for the emphasis on doing 'exactly the same' with substance B, as this is the whole aim of controlled variables.

Answer 2

Measure out 50 cm^3 of water in a beaker. Add solid A until no more dissolves. Filter any undissolved A. Evaporate the solution to see how much of A dissolved. Do exactly the same for substance B making sure you use the same amount of water.

Mark	3	Grade	C

Reasoning: First controlled variable was same volume of water. Second mark was filtering any undissolved A to make a fair comparison. Third mark for emphasising you must do exactly the same for the other substance.

Measure out same volume of water at same temperature in two beakers. Stir solid A in one beaker until no more dissolves. Filter undissolved A and evaporate solution to find how much solid A dissolved.

Do same for substance B in other beaker making sure stir the same number of times

Mark	5		Grade	A

Reasoning: The five controlled variables

1. Same volume of water
2. Same temperature of water as this affects solubility.
3. Stir for same number of times
4. Filter any undissolved substance
5. Did exactly same for other substance as set up two identical beakers.

Step III Test Yourself

1. Select which of these attitudes would be useful during scientific inquiry.

1. Arrogance	2. Flexibility	3. Guesswork	4. Integrity
A. 1, 2 and 3	B. 2 and 3	C. 2 and 4	D. 2, 3 and 4	[1]

2. A good scientist will have the following skills:

   Observing   Inferring   Communicating   Planning

   Match each of the following science activities to **one** of the above skills.

   (a) Recording temperatures ....

   (b) Drawing graphs ....

   (c) Taking photographs with smart phone ....

   (d) Looking for patterns in results ....

   (e) Deciding the order of an investigation ....   [5]

3. A hypothesis is an intelligent guess to explain a particular event or situation. Deduce two possible hypotheses to explain the following:

   (a) Light travels faster than sound.

   1 .... [1]

   2 .... [1]

(b) I never hear my alarm clock on my smart phone in the morning.

1 .... [1]

2 .... [1]

(c) A leaf on a tree went higher up the tree when it first came off.

1 .... [1]

2 .... [1]

MODEL ANSWERS

1. C (Other useful characteristics are curiosity, perseverance, objectivity, open-mindedness, keen observation)   [1]

2. (a) Observing (Using senses to make measurements)

   (b) Communicating (Sharing knowledge and information)

   (c) Communicating

   (d) Inferring (Using results to explain something)

   (e) Planning (Before investigation deciding what to do)   [5]

3. (a) Sound is heavier than light   [1]

   Light has more energy than sound.   [1]

   allow: Answers in reverse i.e. sound has less energy than light

   ignore: Vague answers like 'less resistance on light '

   (b) Alarm is switched off/broken/lost etc.

   I have cotton wool in my ears/pillow over my head etc.

   I get up before the alarm goes off etc.

   allow: Many other possible answers but not too imaginary.
   A maximum of two marks, one for each sensible reason.   [2]

   (c) Squirrel/bird/animal carried the leaf up the tree.

   Gust of wind blew the leaf higher up

   allow: Many other possible answers but not too imaginary.
   A maximum of two marks, one for each sensible reason.   [2]

Physical Properties of Matter

A. Measurement of Length, Volume and Mass
B. Density of a Material
C. Important Physical Properties of Matter
D. Classification of Materials
E. Sustainability of Materials

A. Measurement of Length, Volume and Mass

Step I Key Knowledge

- All measurement is expressed in two parts: the **numerical value** and the **unit.**

- The main **S. I. base units** for measuring length, mass, time and temperature are:

Physical Quantity	S.I. Base Unit
Length	metre (m)
Mass	kilogram (kg)
Time	second (s)
Temperature	Kelvin (K)

- Smaller or larger **multiples of the base unit** are described by adding prefixes.

Prefix	Meaning	Symbol
Nano	One billionth	n
Micro	One millionth	μ
Milli	One thousandth	m
Centi	One hundredth	c
Deci	One tenth	d
Kilo	One thousand	k
Mega	One million	M
Giga	One billion	G

- The **volume** of an object is the **amount of three-dimensional space** the object occupies.

- The **units of volume** are **cm³** (cubic centimetres) or for large volumes **m³** (cubic metres). Other common units, especially for liquids, are **litres** (1000 cm³) and **millilitres** (1 cm³).

- Instruments for **measuring volume** are **measuring cylinder, measuring flask, burette** and **pipette**. The volume is read from the bottom of the **meniscus,** which is the curved surface of the liquid level in the narrow neck of these apparatus.

Common Errors

- Reading an instrument from any angle will give the same reading.

  It does not as parallax errors occur when you read from different angles. Always read the scale of the instrument by looking straight down at 90 degrees to the scale.

- The **volume of irregular objects** can be determined using **displacement methods**. Small irregular objects can be measured by immersing the object completely in a known volume of water in a measuring cylinder. The difference between the volume of water to start and the volume after complete immersion of the object, is the volume of the object.

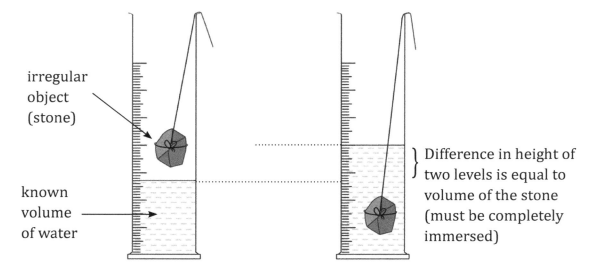

irregular object (stone)

known volume of water

} Difference in height of two levels is equal to volume of the stone (must be completely immersed)

- The **mass** of an object is the **amount of matter** it contains.

- **Matter** is anything that takes up space and has mass. Living matter are plants and animals, non-living matter are rocks, air, water etc.

Step II Be the Teacher

This question is followed by three model answers.

One of these answers is a Grade A answer (above 80% correct), another a Grade C answer (around 50% correct). The third answer could be any grade (A to E).

Mark all three answers giving an appropriate grade with reasoning.

Question

Explain which of the following are classed as matter.

Clouds   Heat   Air   Noise   Water vapour   [6 marks]

Answer 1

Clouds and water vapour are matter as they both can be seen. Heat, air and noise are invisible so they are not matter.

Mark   Grade

Reasoning: ....
....
....
....
....

Answer 2

Clouds, air and water vapour are matter as they can be seen and touched. Heat and noise cannot be touched.

Mark   Grade

Reasoning: ....
....
....
....
....

Answer 3

Only three are matter as they have mass and occupy space. They are clouds, air and water vapour. Noise is sound and along with heat is a form of energy and not a form of matter.

Mark		Grade	

Reasoning: ....
....
....

Actual Mark and Grade for Question

Answer 1

Clouds and water vapour are matter as they both can be seen. Heat, air and noise are invisible so they are not matter.

Mark	2	Grade	D

Reasoning: Two out of three marks for correctly identifying clouds and water as matter (omitted air).

No marks for the correct explanation that matter has mass and occupies space.

Also no mark for saying the other two (heat and noise) are forms of energy.

Answer 2

Clouds, air and water vapour are matter as they can been seen and touched. Heat and noise cannot be touched.

Mark	3	Grade	C

Reasoning: Three marks for the correct identity of the three that are matter (clouds, air, water).

However no marks for the correct explanation that matter has mass and occupies space.

Also no mark for saying other two (heat and noise) are forms of energy.

Answer 3

Only three are matter as they have mass and occupy space. They are clouds, air and water vapour. Noise is sound and along with heat is a form of energy and not a form of matter.

Mark	6	Grade	A

Reasoning: A commendable answer scoring all six marks:

3 marks for correctly identifying clouds, air and water.

2 marks for correctly stating why….because they have mass and occupy space.

1 mark for correctly stating that noise (sound) and heat are energy.

Step III Test Yourself

1. (a) Classify these prefixes in order of **increasing** size.

   kilo-   micro-   mega-   milli-   deci-

   .... [4]

   (b) Calculate how many milligrams there are in 1 metric tonne (1000 kg)

   ....
   ....
   .... [2]

2. The diagrams show the dimensions of three different shaped cubes and cuboids.

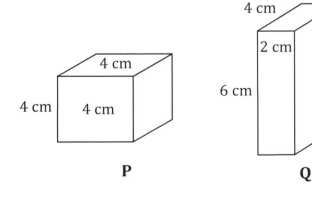

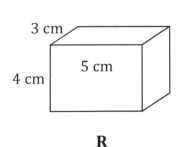

P   Q   R

Calculate the total surface area of each cube/cuboid to decide which has the greatest surface area.

....

....

....

.... [6]

3. The four objects below were each placed in the beaker of water shown.

Wooden block

Aluminium cube

area = 20cm²

volume = 95cm³

Beaker of water

Brass cylinder   **Steel bearing**

Calculate which of these four objects would cause the beaker of water to overflow.

....

....

....

....

....

.... [8]

MODEL ANSWERS

1. (a) micro → milli → deci → kilo → mega [4]
   (lose one mark for each unit in the wrong order)

   (b) 1 tonne = 1000 kg = 1000000 g [1]
   = 1000000 000 mg [1]

2. Surface area of cube P = (4 × 4) × 6 sides [1]

   = 96 cm² [1] (require units for second mark)

   allow: 96 scores 1 mark, 96 cm² with no working scores both marks

   Surface area of cuboid Q = [(6 × 2) × 2 sides] + [(2 × 4) × 2 sides] +

   [(4 × 6) × 2 sides] [1]

   = 88 cm² [1] (require units for second mark)

   allow: 88 scores 1 mark, 88 cm² with no working scores both marks

   Surface area of cuboid R = [(4 × 5) × 2 sides] + [(4 × 3) × 2 sides] +

   [(3 × 5) × 2 sides] [1]

   = 94 cm² [1] (state largest area for second mark)

   allow: 94 scores 1 mark, 94 cm² with no working scores both marks if state largest.

3. For beaker to overflow, the object must sink and have a volume greater than 100 cm³ (the remaining volume in the beaker).

Object	Does it sink	Volume	Conclusion
Wooden block	Floats	5 × 6 × 5 = 150 cm³ [1]	Floats [1]
Aluminium cube	Sinks	5 × 5 × 5 = 125 cm³ [1]	Overflows [1]
Brass cylinder	Sinks	20 × 4 = 80 cm³ [1]	Does not overflow [1]
Steel bearing	Sinks	95 cm³ [1]	Does not overflow [1]

allow: correct volume marks if no units

Total 20 marks

B. Density of Material

Step I Key Knowledge

- The **density** of a substance is its **mass per unit volume**.

- Different materials have different densities as different amounts of matter can be packed into the same volume.

- The density of a substance can be found from the formula

$$\text{Density} = \frac{\text{Mass}}{\text{Volume}} \quad \text{or} \quad D = \frac{m}{V}$$

- The **unit for density** is **grams per cubic centimetre (g/cm³)** or **kilograms per cubic metre (kg/m³)**.

- The density of an object may be calculated by measuring its mass and volume. Then, using the formula, divide its mass by its volume.

- The **density of water is 1 g/cm³**. When the density of a substance (solid or liquid) is greater than that of water it will **sink** in water. If the density of a substance (solid or liquid) is less than that of water it will **float** on water. The substance must not react or dissolve in the water.

Common Errors

- All materials with a density of less than 1 g/cm³ will float in water. Only substances that are insoluble in water, with a density of less than 1 g/cm³ will float. Oil (density 0.9 g/cm³) floats but alcohol (density 0.8 g/cm³) dissolves and does not float.

Step II Be the Teacher

This question is followed by three model answers.

One of these answers is a Grade A answer (above 80% correct), another a Grade C answer (around 50% correct). The third answer could be any grade (A to E).

Mark all three answers giving an appropriate grade with reasoning.

Question 1

Explain why a 10 g piece of cork with a volume of 40 cm³ floats in water but a 5.4 g piece of aluminium of volume 2 cm³ sinks in water.   [6 marks]

Answer 1

The density of an object is given by the formula

$$\text{Density} = \text{mass/volume}$$

The density of cork is therefore $10/40 = 0.25$ but the density of aluminium is $5.4/2 = 2.70$. Aluminium has a heavier density than cork so its sinks but cork floats.

Mark		Grade	

Reasoning: ....
....
....

Answer 2

Cork has a much greater volume so a 10 g piece of cork with a volume of 40 cm³ will float in water but a 5.4 g piece of aluminium of volume 2 cm³ sinks in water. They both have a different density.

Mark		Grade	

Reasoning: ....
....
....

Answer 3

The density of cork is less than the density of water so it floats. The density of aluminium is greater than water so it sinks.

Cork $= 10$ g/40 cm³ $= 0.25$

aluminium $= 5.4$ g/2 cm³ $= 2.7$

Mark		Grade	

Reasoning: ....
....
....

Actual Mark and Grade for Question 1

Answer 1

The density of an object is given by the formula

Density = mass/volume

The density of cork is therefore 10/40 = 0.25 but the density of aluminium is 5.4/2 = 2.70. Aluminium has a heavier density than cork so its sinks but cork floats.

Mark	3		Grade	C

Reasoning: The correct calculation of density is worth 2 marks for each material. However this candidate has not given the units of density (g/cm³) so loses one mark and scores three marks out of four.

The other two marks are also lost for not comparing their densities to water. They need to point out that aluminium has a higher density than water so sinks but cork a lower density than water, so it floats.

Answer 2

Cork has a much greater volume so a 10 g piece of cork with a volume of 40 cm³ will float in water but a 5.4 g piece of aluminium of volume 2 cm³ sinks in water. They both have a different density.

Mark	1		Grade	E

Reasoning: The candidate has mainly just repeated the question. There are no marks allocated for repeating what you have already been told by the examiner. However the candidate does realise they have different densities so scores 1 mark.

Answer 3

The density of cork is less than the density of water so it floats. The density of aluminium is greater than water so it sinks.

Cork = 10 g/40 cm³ = 0.25

aluminium = 5.4 g/2 cm³ = 2.7

Reasoning: Candidate scores 3 marks out of 4 marks for calculation of densities. They lose one mark for not giving the correct unit of density (g/cm^3) in their answer.

They also score another 2 marks for correctly comparing the density of cork and aluminium to water to explain if they float or sink.

Question 2

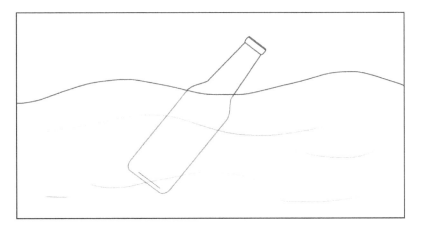

Explain why an empty glass bottle with its spout above the water floats even though the density of glass is greater than water.   [4 marks]

Answer 1

The air inside the bottle lowers the mass of the empty bottle. As the bottle becomes lighter it becomes less dense and floats in the water.

| Mark | | | Grade | |

Reasoning:..
....
....
....
....

Answer 2

The volume of the bottle is increased with the air inside. As the volume increases the density of the bottle decreases as density is mass/volume. The density becomes lower than 1 g/cm³ so the bottle floats in water.

Mark		Grade	

Reasoning: ....
....
....

Answer 3

The density of the empty bottle is its mass (glass + air)/volume (glass + air). For the empty bottle to float in water its density must be below 1g/cm³.

The mass of the glass hardly changes if we add the mass of the air inside the bottle. However adding the volume of air inside the bottle to the volume of the glass increases the total volume a lot. This results in the overall density of the bottle being below 1g/cm³.

Mark		Grade	

Reasoning: ....
....
....

Actual Mark and Grade for Question 2

Answer 1

The air inside the bottle lowers the mass of the empty bottle. As the bottle becomes lighter it becomes less dense and floats in the water.

Mark	0	Grade	E

Reasoning: The mass of the glass and air inside is the mass of the empty bottle. Air does not lower the mass of the empty bottle. Not having any liquid inside and replacing the liquid with air lowers the mass and makes an empty bottle lighter and less dense than a full bottle.

Answer 2

The volume of the bottle is increased with the air inside. As the volume increases the density of the empty bottle decreases as density is mass/volume. The density becomes lower than 1 g/cm³ so the bottle floats in water.

Mark	2		Grade	C

Reasoning: The volume of the bottle does not change having air inside. The combined volume of the glass and the volume of the air is what increases.

However 1 mark for relating to overall density = mass/volume. Also 1 mark for identifying overall density must be lower than 1 g/cm³ for the bottle to float in water.

Answer 3

The density of the empty bottle is its mass (glass + air)/volume (glass + air). For the empty bottle to float in water its density must be below 1g/cm³.

The mass of the glass hardly changes if we add the mass of the air inside the bottle. However adding the volume of air inside the bottle to the volume of the glass increase the total volume a lot. This result in the overall density of the bottle being below 1g/cm³.

Mark	4		Grade	A

Reasoning: Excellent answer, very clearly and accurately explained.

1 mark for relating to overall density = overall mass (glass + air) / overall volume (glass + air).

1 mark for identifying overall density must be lower than 1 g/cm³ for the bottle to float in water.

1 mark for saying overall mass hardly increases at all with the mass of the air included.

1 mark for saying overall volume increases a lot if we add the volume of air to the volume of the glass.

Step III Test Yourself

1. A small iceberg has a volume of 80 m³ and a mass of 73 600 kg.

    (a) Calculate the density of ice in kg/m³?

    ....

    .... [3]

    (b) Calculate the density of ice in g/cm³?

    ....

    .... [2]

    (c) Explain why ice floats on water.

    .... [1]

2. Explain what happens to the density of water when water evaporates from a puddle and becomes water vapour.

    ....

    ....

    .... [3]

3.

Using the above diagrams deduce the density of the alcohol.

    ....

    ....

    .... [3]

MODEL ANSWERS

1. (a) Density = Mass / Volume [1]

    = 73 600 kg / 80 m³ [1]

    = 920 kg/m³ [1] (must have units for the third mark)

   (b) Density = 1000 kg/m³ = 1 g/cm³ [1]

    = 920 kg/m³ = 0.92 g/cm³ [1]

   allow: 0.92 would score 1 mark

   (c) Ice floats on water as its density (0.92 g/cm³) is less than water (1 g/cm³). [1]

   allow: ice density less or mass per unit volume less both score 1 mark

   ignore: ice lighter

2. When water evaporates from a puddle the water molecules become further apart, so its volume increases. [1]

   allow: volume increase for 1 mark

   The mass of the molecules remains the same. [1]

   allow: same mass for 1 mark

   Therefore the density of the water vapour becomes less. [1]

   allow: lower density for 1 mark

   ignore: water vapour becomes lighter

3. Volume of alcohol = 25 cm³ [1]

   Mass of alcohol = 205g −185 g = 20 g [1]

   allow: do not have to show working to score this mark

   Density = mass/volume = 20 g/25 cm³ = 0.8 g/cm³ [1]

   allow: do not have to show working to score this mark but must have correct units

   ignore: 0.8 with no unit would not score this third mark

Total 12 marks

C. Important Physical Properties of Matter

Step I Key Knowledge

- **Matter** is all around us and is defined as **any substance or material that occupies space and has mass**.

- When describing the type of material or matter used in making various objects, it is necessary to consider the **physical properties** of the material. Here are some common physical properties and their definitions:

> ➤ **Strength**   Ability to support heavy loads without breaking or tearing.
>
> ➤ **Durability**   Durable materials are long lasting and do not corrode.
>
> ➤ **Lustre**   Shiny materials like metals have lustre.
>
> ➤ **Hardness**   Ability to withstand scratches and wear.
>
> ➤ **Malleable**   Material that can be flattened into sheet form (metals).
>
> ➤ **Ductility**   Material that can be drawn into wire form (metals).
>
> ➤ **Transparency**   See-through materials like glass.
>
> ➤ **Elasticity**   How far a material will stretch without breaking.
>
> ➤ **Density**   The mass per unit volume of the material.
>
> ➤ **Solubility**   Amount of a substance that will dissolve in a certain volume of liquid.
>
> ➤ **Melting point**   The lowest temperature at which all of a solid changes into a liquid.
>
> ➤ **Freezing point**   The highest temperature at which all of a liquid changes into a solid.
>
> ➤ **Boiling point**   The lowest temperature at which all of a liquid changes to a gas.
>
> ➤ **Thermal conductivity**   A measure of how readily heat passes through a material.
>
> ➤ **Electrical conductivity**   A measure of how readily electricity passes through a material.

Common Errors

- Hard materials like metals are durable.

  This is untrue as many metals corrode and rust. Durable means long lasting and such materials must be unreactive. Examples of durable materials are plastics as these are non-biodegradable (cannot be broken down naturally). Some plastics are soft materials but they are still very durable.

Step II Be the Teacher

This question is followed by three model answers.

One of these answers is a Grade A answer (above 80% correct), another a Grade C answer (around 50% correct). The third answer could be any grade (A to E).

Mark all three answers giving an appropriate grade with reasoning.

Question

	Melting point (°C)	Density (g/cm³)	Electrical conductivity
Aluminium	660	2.7	0.382
Copper	1083	8.9	0.593

State three properties of metals which makes them a suitable material for making electrical wire. Also with the help of the above table explain why aluminium metal is chosen for overhead cables and not copper wire which is a better electrical conductor? [4 marks]

Answer 1

Metal wires can't be broken. They are strong and tough materials. Aluminium is used for overhead cables as it is a lighter metal than copper.

Mark [ ]   Grade [ ]

Reasoning:..
....
....

Answer 2

Metals are malleable and ductile. They also are good conductors of heat and electricity with high melting points. From the table aluminium has a lower density than copper so is lighter and the aluminium cable will not sag as much as a copper cable.

Mark		Grade	

Reasoning:..

....

....

Answer 3

The properties of metals which make them suitable for making wires are they last a long time and are easy to cover with plastic. Aluminium is used for overhead cables and not copper wire as it is shiny and white so it is easier for birds or other flying things to see.

Mark		Grade	

Reasoning:..

....

....

Actual Mark and Grade for Question

Answer 1

Metal wires can't be broken. They are strong and tough materials. Aluminium is used for overhead cables as it is a lighter metal than copper.

Mark	2	Grade	C

Reasoning: One out of three marks for the suitable properties of metals. Strong, tough and not broken are the same acceptable property and scores one mark.

Acceptable properties of metals which make them suitable for wiring are: ductile (drawn into wires) / strength / hardness /high melting point /good electrical conductors.

The mark of 'lightness' for why aluminium is chosen over copper is scored.

Answer 2

Metals are malleable and ductile. They also are good conductors of heat and electricity with high melting points. From the table aluminium has a lower density than copper so is lighter and the aluminium cable will not sag as much as a copper cable.

Mark	4		Grade	A

Reasoning: Three marks are scored for the three relevant properties of ductile, good electrical conductor and high melting point. No marks are deducted for the other properties mentioned which are also true but not relevant.

A mark is given for a very good explanation of why aluminium is chosen over copper even though copper is a better conductor.

Answer 3

The properties of metals which make them suitable for making wires are they last a long time and are easy to cover with plastic. Aluminium is used for overhead cables and not copper wire as it is shiny and white so it is easier for birds or other flying things to see.

Mark	0		Grade	E

Reasoning: No marks are scored.

The candidate has copied the question out which scores no marks and their additional sections are perhaps true but not relevant.

The three properties we are looking for are either: ductile (drawn into wires) / strength / hardness /high melting point /good electrical conductor. The low density of aluminium is the key factor for its choice over copper, not its appearance.

Step III Test Yourself

1. Draw a line from the physical property to its correct definition.

Physical Property		Definition	
Ability to allow heat to pass through	•	• Hardness	
Ability to withstand scratching	•	• Durability	
How long a material lasts	•	• Ductility	
Ability of material to be drawn into wire-form	•	• Conductivity	[4]

2. (a) State *two* physical properties of the metal gold which make it suitable for making medals.

    ....

    .... [2]

    (b) State *two* physical properties of the metal steel which make it suitable for making the body of a car.

    ....

    .... [2]

3. Identify the relevant physical property of the material in the following situations.

    (a) Squashing of a foam cushion when sitting on it.

    .... [1]

    (b) Light reflecting off a door handle.

    .... [1]

    (c) Ice cream softening in your mouth.

    .... [1]

    (d) Light passing through a glass ornament.

    .... [1]

MODEL ANSWERS

1. Ability to allow heat to pass through   •   • Hardness [1]

    Ability to withstand scratching   •   • Durability [1]

    How long a material lasts   •   • Ductility [1]

    Ability of material to be drawn into wire-form   •   • Conductivity [1]

2. (a) **allow:** shiny or lustrous, durable or long lasting, hard or not scratched, malleable or easy to shape (any two) [2]

    ignore: looks good, expensive

    (b) **allow:** malleable or easy to shape, strong or hard [2]

    ignore: shiny, lustrous, durable, cheap, ductile

3. (a) elastic   [1]   (b) lustrous or shiny   [1]

    (c) low melting point   [1]   (d) transparent   [1]

    ignore: do not accept any alternatives for these properties

    Total 12 marks

D. Classification of Materials

Step I Key Knowledge

- There are **five main groups** of materials.

Group	Physical Properties	Uses
Metals	Can be shaped into sheets or wires. Shiny and good conductors of heat and electricity	Car bodies, cutlery, coinage, medals, wire, drills, engines
Ceramics	Very hard but brittle. High melting points. Do not corrode and are poor conductors of heat/electricity	Kitchenware, cups, saucers, ornaments, bricks
Glass	Transparent and brittle. Poor conductor of heat and electricity.	Laboratory equipment, windows, mirrors, bottles
Plastics	Easily moulded and shaped. Light and do not corrode.	Containers, bags, cling-film, drink bottles, insulating materials
Fibres	Easily drawn into fine threads. Can be woven and spun and will absorb dyes.	Clothing, rope, curtains, carpets

Common Errors

- Most plastic materials are transparent as they allow light to pass through.

  This is only true of clear plastic. Coloured plastic lets light pass through but diffuses (scatters) the light. Coloured plastic is described as translucent and is not transparent. It has the same effect as looking through obscure glass

- Another method of classification is to group materials according to their **physical state** at room temperature. The classification is either as a **solid, liquid** or **gas**. Most of the main groups of materials (metals, glass, ceramics, plastics and fibres) are solids. The exception is the metal mercury, which is a liquid.

- To be classified as a **solid** a material must have both its **melting and boiling point above room temperature**.

- To be classified as a **liquid** a material must have its **boiling point above room temperature but its melting point below room temperature**.

- To be classified as a **gas** a material must have both **its melting and boiling point below room temperature**.

Common Errors

- A vapour is a gas.....This is not strictly true. A vapour has a boiling point above room temperature but a gas has a boiling point below room temperature. For this reason oxygen is a gas and not a vapour. However it is water vapour and not gaseous water.

Step II Be the Teacher

This question is followed by three model answers.

One of these answers is a Grade A answer (above 80% correct), another a Grade C answer (around 50% correct). The third answer could be any grade (A to E).

Mark all three answers giving an appropriate grade with reasoning.

Question

Materials can be classified according to their physical state.

Identify which of these metals can be distinguished from the other metals because of its state?

Sodium   Gold   Silver   Chromium   Mercury   [2 marks]

Answer 1

Sodium metal is much more reactive than the other metals so it melts more easily.

Mark [   ]   Grade [   ]

Reasoning: ....
....

Answer 2

Mercury as it has the highest melting point.

Mark [   ]   Grade [   ]

Reasoning: ....
....

Answer 3

Mercury as it is a liquid at room temperature the others are solids.

Mark		Grade	

Reasoning: ....

....

Actual Mark and Grade for Question

Answer 1

Sodium metal is much more reactive than the other metals so it melts more easily.

Mark	0	Grade	E

Reasoning: No marks are scored.

Sodium is the most chemically reactive of the five metals and it does have a low melting point (97°C). However mercury is a liquid at room temperature (melting point is – 39°C) and the question asked to classify with respect to physical state not chemical reactivity.

Answer 2

Mercury as it has the highest melting point.

Mark	1	Grade	C

Reasoning: Chose the correct metal but has the lowest melting point (-39°C) and is a liquid at room temperature.

Answer 3

Mercury as it is a liquid at room temperature the others are solids.

Mark	2	Grade	A

Reasoning: Both marks are scored.

First mark is choosing the correct metal

Second mark is identifying it as a liquid (lowest melting point) at room temperature while the others are solid at room temperature.

Step III Test Yourself

1. Consider the five common classes of material

    Plastic   Metal   Fibre   Ceramic   Glass

    Choose the most suitable class of material to make the following five objects. Each class of material can only be used once. When you have decided which material to use give **one physical property** which makes it suitable.

Drinking mug   **Shirt**   **Wine bottle**

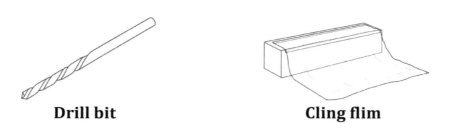

Drill bit   **Cling flim**

(a) Drinking mug

.... [2]

(b) Shirt

.... [2]

(c) Wine bottle

.... [2]

(d) Drill bit

.... [2]

(e) Cling film

.... [2]

2. The table shows the melting and boiling point of three materials. Classify these materials in terms of their physical state at room temperature (25 °C). Explain your classification.

Material	Melting point (°C)	Boiling point (°C)
P	+ 32	+63
Q	−6	+15
R	+10	+84

P .... [2]

Q .... [2]

R .... [2]

MODEL ANSWERS

1. (a) Drinking mug ceramic [1] as high melting point [1]

   allow: unreactive, not corrode, poor heat conductor

   ignore: hard, colourful, poor conductor of electricity

   (b) Shirt is fibre [1] as easily drawn into thread [1]

   allow: can be woven/spun, flexible

   ignore: colourful, light

   (c) Wine bottle is glass [1] as transparent [1]

   ignore: clear, high melting point, unreactive, poor conductor

   (d) Drill bit is metal [1] as strong or hard [1]

   allow: tough

   ignore: durable, good conductor, high density

   (e) Cling film is plastic [1] as flexible or transparent [1]

   ignore: unreactive, light

2. P is solid [1] as both melting and boiling points are above room temperature. [1]
   Q is gas [1] as both melting and boiling points are below room temperature. [1]
   R is liquid [1] as melting point is below but boiling point is above room temperature. [1]

Total 16 marks

E. Sustainability of Materials

Step I Key Knowledge

- Supplies of certain **fossil fuels** (coal, oil and natural gas) and metal reserves will **run out** within the foreseeable future.

- In order to **conserve** such valuable resources we need to **practise the 3Rs:** reduce, reuse, recycle.

- If you **reduce** usage and find alternative materials then this will conserve reserves of that material.

- If you **reuse** the existing material instead of making new material then this will conserve reserves of that material.

- If you **recycle** a material then the raw material it is made from is saved for later use. Recycling materials like **glass, metal, paper, fibre and plastic** is very important and helps to make such materials more sustainable.

- **Recycling** materials like paper helps to **reduce the destruction of forests**. This has environmental impact as it **lessens global warming**.

- **Recycling** plastics helps **conserve fossil fuels,** like crude oil from which plastics are made. It also has an environmental impact as many **plastics are non-biodegradable** (not broken down naturally) and therefore such plastics can cause land pollution.

- **Disposal of harmful material** will impact on the environment unless the material has been **treated first**. Sewage must be treated before it is discharged into rivers or the sea.

Common Errors

- Recycle and reuse are the same thing...they are not.

  You can recycle a newspaper but you cannot reuse it. Recycling a glass bottle means melting the bottle to make a new bottle or new glass object. Reusing a glass bottle means washing out the bottles and refilling it.

Step II Be the Teacher

This question is followed by three model answers.

One of these answers is a Grade A answer (above 80% correct), another a Grade C answer (around 50% correct). The third answer could be any grade (A to E).

Mark all three answers giving an appropriate grade with reasoning.

Question

Compare recycling and reusing. Identify two advantages of recycling or reusing a material instead of making new material from raw materials. **[4 marks]**

Answer 1

Recycling involves modifying an existing material, so that is used again. Reusing is just cleaning a material, like a bottle, so that it can be reused. Both of these save raw materials and save energy from making a new object from scratch.

Mark		Grade	

Reasoning:..
....
....

Answer 2

Reusing involves just refilling but recycling involves putting it back onto a machine. Both of these are cheaper than making something from scratch.

Mark		Grade	

Reasoning:..
....
....

Answer 3

Recycling differs from reusing as it takes longer. However they are both quicker than making from raw material and is cheaper and saves energy.

Mark		Grade	

Reasoning:..
....
....

Actual Mark and Grade for Question

Answer 1

Recycling involves modifying an existing material, so that is used again. Reusing is just cleaning a material, like a bottle, so that it can be reused. Both of these save raw materials and save energy from making a new object from scratch.

| Mark | 4 | Grade | A |

Reasoning: A commendable answer covering all four marking points.

First two marks are for correctly distinguishing the two processes. Recycling involves modifying the material but reusing involves just cleaning.

Two marks for advantages chosen from the following:
Saves energy (fossil fuels) / saves natural resources (raw materials) / saves time / cheaper

Answer 2

Reusing involves just refilling but recycling involves putting it back onto a machine. Both of these are cheaper than making something from scratch.

| Mark | 1 | Grade | D |

Reasoning: No marks for distinguishing refilling and recycling. Recycling involves modifying the material but reusing involves just cleaning.

One mark for saying both (recycling/reusing) is cheaper than making from scratch (raw materials).

Answer 3

Recycling differs from reusing as it takes longer. However they are both quicker than making from raw material and is cheaper and saves energy.

| Mark | 2 | Grade | C |

Reasoning: No marks for distinguishing refilling and recycling. Recycling involves modifying the material but reusing involves just cleaning.

Two marks for saying cheaper and saves energy. Could argue saving energy is the main reason it is cheaper, but you also save raw materials, and labour which are also cost related.

Step III Test Yourself

1. State which of these **cannot** be recycled? Explain your choice.

    Metal cans   Food   Waste paper   Petrol

    ....

    ....

    ....

    .... [4]

2. Explain how recycling material can lessen global warming.

    ....

    ....

    .... [2]

(MODEL ANSWERS)

1. Petrol [1] cannot be recycled because once used as a fuel it changes chemically
    [1] into gases [1] which escape into the air [1].
    ignore: petrol is a liquid, petrol escapes, petrol changes

2. Recycling material lessens global warming as less fossil fuels need to be used
    [1]. This is because manufacture of goods/materials often uses heat/electricity
    which are energy forms produced from fossil fuels. [1]
    allow: recycling uses less fossil fuels, recycling uses less energy
    ignore: recycling is cheaper.

Chemical Composition of Matter

A. Elements and the Periodic Table

B. Properties of Metals and Non-Metals

C. Compounds and Mixtures

D. Solutions and Suspensions

A. Elements and the Periodic Table

Step I Key Knowledge

- All **living and non-living matter** consist of basic units called **elements**.

- An **element** is a substance which **cannot be broken down into two or more simpler substances by chemical means**.

- Most **elements** occur **combined** with other elements. For example, the element hydrogen mainly occurs combined with the element oxygen in the form of water.

- All known elements are arranged in a chart called the **Periodic Table**.

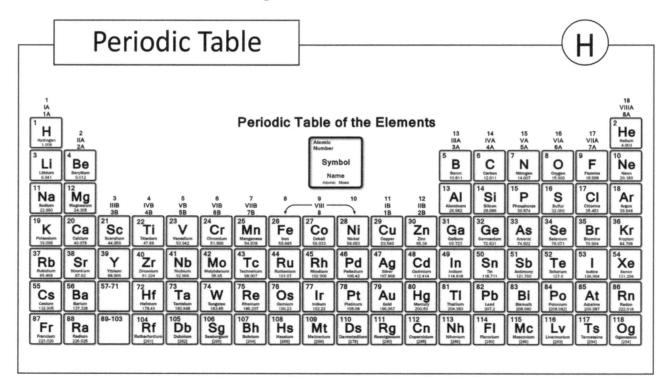

- Every element is represented by a **chemical symbol**. For example, oxygen is represented by O and hydrogen by the symbol H.

Common Errors

- CL is the chemical symbol for chlorine gas.

  This is wrong as all chemical symbols have a small letter for the second letter (Cl), only a capital letter for the first letter. Also Cl is chemical symbol for an atom of the element. Chlorine gas is a molecule of the element and has a chemical formula (not symbol) of Cl_2.

- Each **vertical column** in the Periodic Table is called a **group**. Elements within a group have similar chemical properties.

- Each **horizontal** row in the Periodic Table is called a **period**. The elements, as we go from left to right across the period, change from solid metals to liquid or gaseous non-metals.

Step II Be the Teacher

This question is followed by three model answers.

One of these answers is a Grade A answer (above 80% correct), another a Grade C answer (around 50% correct). The third answer could be any grade (A to E).

Mark all three answers giving an appropriate grade with reasoning.

Question

Classify which of these materials are elements. Explain your choice.

Iron   Steel   Chlorine   Copper   Salt   Water   Gold   [5 marks]

Answer 1

Iron, steel, copper and gold are elements as they are all metals and contain only one type of atom.

Mark [ ]   Grade [ ]

Reasoning:..
....
....
....
....

Answer 2

Iron, steel and copper are elements as they are extracted from ores.

| Mark | | Grade | |

Reasoning: ....
....
....
....

Answer 3

Iron, chlorine, copper and gold are all elements as they all contain only one type of atom. Steel, salt and water contain different elements so are compounds.

| Mark | | Grade | |

Reasoning: ....
....
....
....

Actual Mark and Grade for Question

Answer 1

Iron, steel, copper and gold are elements as they are all metals and contain only one type of atom.

| Mark | 3 | Grade | C |

Reasoning: The correct identification of three elements (iron, copper and gold) scores three marks but the incorrectly chosen 'steel element' loses one of these marks. So there are 2 out of a possible 4 marks scored

The correct explanation of containing only one type of atom scores 1 mark

Answer 2

Iron, steel and copper are elements as they are extracted from ores and contain only atoms. ✓

| Mark | 1 |

| Grade | E |

Reasoning: The correct identification of the four elements (iron, copper, chlorine and gold) scores four marks but each incorrectly chosen element loses one mark.

As steel was incorrectly chosen there is 1 mark out of 4 scored.

Need to say only one type of atom in elements to score the explanation mark.

Answer 3

Iron, chlorine, copper and gold are all elements as they all contain only one type of atom. Steel, salt and water contain different elements so are compounds. ✓ ✓ ✓

| Mark | 5 |

| Grade | A |

Reasoning: All four elements (iron, copper, chlorine and gold) are correctly identified to score four marks.

The explanation mark of only one type of atom is also scored, so the student scores full marks. Steel, salt and water do contain different elements but only water and salt are compounds where the different elements are chemically combined. Steel is a mixture (alloy) where there is no chemical combination between the different elements. However as there is only one mark for the explanation it would be unfair to penalise the student.

Step III Test Yourself

1. Consider **only the elements** identified by their chemical symbol **in the outline** of the top part of the Periodic Table shown below.

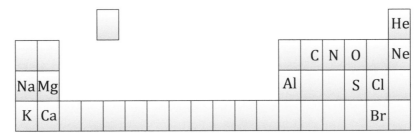

(a) How many of the 13 identified elements are metals?

....[1]

(b) Identify the chemical names of the four non-metallic elements shown in Period-2.

....

....[4]

(c) Identify the chemical names of the two metallic elements shown in Group 2.

....[2]

(d) Identify the chemical names of four elements shown, which are gases at room temperature.

....

....[4]

2. (a) A solid element is dull and brittle and makes no sound when it is hit. Underline which of these four elements you think it is, explaining your choice.

Magnesium   Aluminium   Potassium   Sulfur

....[2]

(b) A solid element has a high electrical conductivity and can be can be hammered into flat sheets. Underline which of these four elements you think it is, explaining your choice.

Iodine   Phosphorus   Magnesium   Sulfur

....[2]

MODEL ANSWERS

1. (a) 5 [1]

(b) carbon [1] nitrogen [1] oxygen [1] neon [1]

allow: incorrect spelling as long as chemical name sounds similar when pronounced

(c) magnesium [1] calcium [1]

allow: incorrect spelling

(d) Any four from helium, nitrogen, oxygen, neon, or chlorine [4]

2. (a) Sulfur [1] as has these properties of a non-metal [1]

allow: sulfur [1] is non-metal [1]

(b) Magnesium [1] as has these properties of a metal [1]

allow: magnesium [1] is metal [1]

Total 15 marks

B. Properties of Metals and Non-Metals

Step I Key Knowledge

- Elements in the Periodic Table can be classified into **metals** and **non-metals** according to their different **physical properties**.

Metals	Non-metals
• Good conductor of heat	• Poor conductor of heat
• Good electrical conductor	• Poor electrical conductor
• Can be pulled into wires (ductile)	• Non-ductile
• Can be beaten into shape (malleable)	• Brittle and snap easily
• Give a ringing sound (sonorous)	• Not sonorous
• Shiny appearance (lustrous)	• Dull appearance
• High densities	• Low densities

Common Errors

- All metals are shiny, malleable solids... not quite.

  Mercury is an exception and is a liquid at room temperature and pressure.

Step II Be the Teacher

This question is followed by three model answers.

One of these answers is a Grade A answer (above 80% correct), another a Grade C answer (around 50% correct). The third answer could be any grade (A to E).

Mark all three answers giving an appropriate grade with reasoning.

List four ways how you could confirm that an unknown element was a metal and not a non-metal. [4 marks]

Answer 1

The unknown element should be a good conductor of electricity. It should also be tough, strong, shiny and hard.

Mark [ ]   Grade [ ]

Reasoning: ....
....
....

Answer 2

Metals have the following properties:

1. Good conductors of heat and electricity
2. Can be hammered into sheets
3. Can be drawn into wires
4. Are shiny

Mark [ ]   Grade [ ]

Reasoning: ....
....
....

Answer 3

Metals are found on the left-hand side of the Periodic Table. If it was a non-metal it would be found on the right-hand side of the Periodic Table.

Mark [ ]   Grade [ ]

Reasoning: ....
....

Actual Mark and Grade for Question

Answer 1

The unknown element should be a good conductor ✓ of electricity. It should also be tough, strong, shiny ✓ and hard.

Mark	2		Grade	C

Reasoning: Good conductor of electricity and shiny scores two marks.

Tough, strong and hard are the same property and there are exceptions like sodium or potassium metals are soft and mercury metal is a liquid. These descriptive terms for metals do not score.

Answer 2

Metals have the following properties:
1. Good conductors of heat and electricity. ✓
2. Can be hammered into sheets ✓
3. Can be drawn into wires ✓
4. Are shiny ✓

Mark	4		Grade	A

Reasoning: It is a good idea in answering questions to make a list. It makes it easier for the examiner to mark and identifies an answer for each of the four marks.

Each of the four properties listed scores a mark. It would also be acceptable to use the words malleable (hammered into sheets) or ductile (drawn into wires) or lustrous (shiny).

Answer 3

Metals are found on the left-hand side of the Periodic Table. If it was a non-metal it would be found on the right-hand side of the Periodic Table.

Mark	0		Grade	E

Reasoning: It is very important that the student answers the question which asks for ways to confirm that an unknown element was a metal. This involves testing the element. If it is unknown you cannot look on the Periodic Table to find out its position.

Step III Test Yourself

1. The properties of four elements are shown in the table.

Element	Ductility	Malleability	Thermal Conductivity	State (25°C)	Colour
1	Good	Good	Very good	Solid	Reddish-brown
2	Poor	Poor	Poor	Liquid	Reddish-brown
3	Poor	Poor	Poor	Solid	Yellow
4	Poor	Poor	Good	Liquid	Silvery

Deduce if the element is a metal or non-metal, giving your reasons.

Element 1 ....
....[2]

Element 2 ....
....[2]

Element 3 ....
....[2]

Element 4 ....
....[2]

2. Alloys are mixtures of metals. For example the alloy brass is a mixture of 70% copper and 30% zinc by mass. Explain how these two metals could be mixed together in their correct proportions to make this alloy.

....
....
....
....[4]

MODEL ANSWERS

1. Element 1 is metal [1] as very good thermal conductivity. [1]
   allow: ductile, malleable or saying metal is copper
   ignore: solid
   Element 2 is non-metal [1] as poor thermal conductivity. [1]
   allow: poor ductility, poor malleability or saying non-metal is bromine
   ignore: liquid

Element 3 is non-metal [1] as poor thermal conductivity. [1]

allow: poor ductility, poor malleability or saying non-metal is sulfur

ignore: solid

Element 4 is metal [1] as good thermal conductivity. [1]

allow: silvery or saying metal is mercury

2. Weigh [1] 7 g of copper and 3 g of zinc. [1]

Then heat mixture so becomes molten. [1]

Stir the mixture [1] then allow to cool.

allow: any correct mass ratio of 7:3 eg 70 g copper 30 g zinc

ignore: heat mixture (must say become molten)

Total 12 marks

C. Compounds and Mixtures

Step I Key Knowledge

- A *compound* is a substance made when *two or more different elements chemically combine together*.

- A *mixture* consists of *two or more substances that are not chemically combined together*. The substances in a mixture may be either elements or compounds.

Compound	Mixture
• A chemical reaction occurs when a compound is formed.	• No chemical reaction occurs when a mixture is formed.
• During a chemical reaction, heat and/ or light is take in or given out.	• Heat or light are not produced when mixtures are formed.
• The properties of a compound are different from the properties of the elements from which it is made.	• A mixture has the properties of the substances that are present in it.
• A compound can only be broken down into simpler substances by chemical means.	• A mixture can be easily separated by physical means.
• The different elements in a compound conbine together in a fixed proportion by mass.	• The substances in a mixture are not present in a fixed proportion.

Common Errors

- Compounds have a chemical formula but mixtures do not have a chemical formula. This is only partly true.

  The elements in a compound are in a fixed proportion by mass so a compound can be represented by a chemical formula. However each component of a mixture can also be represented by a chemical formula. The overall mixture itself does not have a chemical formula as its components are not present in fixed proportions.

Step II Be the Teacher

This question is followed by three model answers.

One of these answers is a Grade A answer (above 80% correct), another a Grade C answer (around 50% correct). The third answer could be any grade (A to E).

Mark all three answers giving an appropriate grade with reasoning.

Question

Explain the difference between a mixture and a compound by comparing the properties of pure water with that of air.   **[6 marks]**

Answer 1

Air is a mixture because its lots of different gases mixed together. Water is a compound as it has different elements. Water is also a compound as it can react chemically with other elements like sodium metal.

Mark [   ]   Grade [   ]

Reasoning: ....
....
....
....

Answer 2

Air is a mixture as its composition can vary and its components can be separated by physical means. Air is not made by a chemical reaction and its properties are those of its components.

Water is a compound as it has a chemical formula (H_2O) and it is difficult to separate the hydrogen and oxygen. It is a liquid and not a mixture of hydrogen and oxygen gases so when it is formed it is a new compound with its own special chemical formula.

Mark		Grade	
			D

Reasoning: ....

....

....

Answer 3

Air is a mixture as the gases in the air are not chemically combined. Water is the compound as it is a chemical with the hydrogen and oxygen chemically combined.

Mark		Grade	

Reasoning: ....

....

....

....

Actual Mark and Grade for Question

Answer 1

Air is a mixture because its lots of different gases mixed together. Water is a compound as it has different elements. Water is also a compound as it can react chemically with other elements like sodium metal.

Mark		Grade	
	2		D

Reasoning: The student scores two marks for correctly identifying air as the mixture and water as the compound.

No other marks were scored as air also has different elements (mainly oxygen, nitrogen). The oxygen in the air will also chemically react with sodium to form sodium oxide.

Air is a mixture as its composition can vary and its components can be separated by physical means. Air is not made by a chemical reaction and its properties are those of its components.

Water is a compound as it has a chemical formula (H_2O) and it is difficult to separate the hydrogen and oxygen. It is a liquid and not a mixture of hydrogen and oxygen gases so when it is formed it is a new compound with its own special chemical formula.

Mark	6		Grade	A

Reasoning: The student scores two marks for correctly identifying air as the mixture and water as the compound.

The student also scores the remaining four marks by correctly pointing out four properties of mixtures/compounds.

- Mixtures composition varies but compounds have a fixed composition (chemical formula).
- Can separate components of mixture by physical means. Can only separate components of compound by chemical means.
- When a mixture forms there is no chemical reaction. When a compound forms there is a chemical reaction (energy change)
- A mixture has the properties of its components. A compound has its own individual properties, different from its component elements.

Air is a mixture as the gases in the air are not chemically combined. Water is the compound as it is a chemical with the hydrogen and oxygen chemically combined.

Mark	3		Grade	C

Reasoning: The student scores two marks for correctly identifying air as the mixture and water as the compound.

The student scores one other mark for saying that in mixtures there is no chemical combination between components but in compounds there is chemical combination.

The three missing marks are

- Mixtures composition varies but compounds have a fixed composition (chemical formula).

- Can separate components of mixture by physical means. Can only separate a components of compound by chemical means.

- A mixture has the properties of its components. A compound has its own individual properties, different from its component elements.

Step III Test Yourself

1. One substance is different from the other three as it is a mixture and the other three are compounds or vice versa. Underline the odd one out explaining your choice.

   (a) Petrol   Methane   Diesel   Paraffin

   ....
   .... [2]

   (b) Beer   Wine   Cider   Alcohol

   ....
   .... [2]

   (c) Salt   Distilled water   Sea water   Rain water

   ....
   .... [2]

2. This question is concerned with the compound(s) formed by chemical reactions of magnesium metal. Match the chemicals reacted to the correct compound formed by drawing a line between the two.

Chemicals reacted	Compound(s) formed
Burning magnesium in air ●	● Magnesium sulfide
Adding magnesium to sulfuric acid ●	● Magnesium sulfate (and copper)
Heating magnesium and sulfur together ●	● Magnesium oxide
Adding magnesium to aqueous copper sulfate ●	● Magnesium sulfate (and hydrogen)

   [4]

3. 'When a compound is formed from its elements, the properties of the compound are completely different from the elements it is made from.'

Explain this statement by using the example of heating the element copper in oxygen gas (air) to form the compound copper oxide.

....

....

....

....[4]

4. A silvery substance X when heated in air (oxygen) caught alight and formed a white ash Y. A substance Z when heated strongly gave off carbon dioxide gas and left the white solid Y. Decide if X, Y and Z are elements or compounds giving your reasons.

X .... [2]

Y .... [2]

Z .... [2]

MODEL ANSWERS

1. (a) Methane [1] as compound. [1]
   allow: Others (petrol, diesel, paraffin) are mixtures.

   (b) Alcohol [1] as compound. [1]
   allow: Others (beer, wine, cider) are mixtures.

   (c) Sea water [1] as mixture. [1]
   allow: Others (salt, distilled water, rain water) are compounds.

2.

Burning magnesium in air		Magnesium sulfide [1]
Adding magnesium to sulfuric acid		Magnesium sulfate (and copper) [1]
Heating magnesium and sulfur together		Magnesium oxide [1]
Adding magnesium to aqueous copper sulfate		Magnesium sulfate (and hydrogen) [1]

3. Copper is metal and a good conductor. [1] Copper oxide is a non-conductor. [1]

   allow: other metallic properties of copper compared to the lack of such properties in copper oxide.

   Oxygen is a gas. [1] Copper oxide is a black solid. [1]

   allow: other comparisons of non-metallic properties with copper oxide.

4. X is an element [1] as undergoes chemical reaction with oxygen (air). [1]

   allow: X is magnesium, X is metal

   Y is compound [1] as burning of X means oxygen combines with X. [1]

   allow: white ash is oxide/magnesium oxide

   Z is compound [1] as gives off carbon dioxide on heating. [1]

   allow: undergoes decomposition/thermal decomposition, Z is magnesium carbonate

   Total 20 marks

D. Solutions and Suspensions

Step I Key Knowledge

- A **solution** contains a dissolved substance called the **solute**, in a liquid called the **solvent**. The resulting mixture of solute and solvent is called a solution.

- For example, in sugar solution, sugar is the solute and water is the solvent. An **aqueous solution** is a solution containing water as the solvent.

$$\textbf{Solute} \ + \ \textbf{Solvent} \ \rightarrow \ \textbf{Solution}$$

$$\text{Sugar} \ + \ \text{Water} \ \rightarrow \ \text{Sugar solution}$$

- A solution is a **homogenous mixture**. This means that its colour, density, appearance and other properties are the same in every part of the solution.

- At a certain temperature, only a certain amount of solute will dissolve in a particular volume of solvent. This is known as the **solubility** of the solute. It normally increases with increasing temperature.

- The **three factors** that speed up the rate of dissolving are:

  1. **Temperature**. Normally, the higher the temperature, the faster the solute will dissolve.

  2. **Rate of stirring**. The solute will dissolve faster if it is stirred quickly.

  3. **Size of solute particles**. The smaller the size of the solute particles, the quicker the solute will dissolve. Grinding solutes into powder form increases the surface area of the solute so that it will dissolve faster.

- **A suspension** is a **mixture** containing an **insoluble fine-particled solid in a liquid** (or a gas). Examples of suspensions include calamine lotion and muddy water.

Solution	Suspension
• When left to settle the solute particles do not separate from the solvent particles. • It forms a **homogenous mixture**. • Its parts cannot be separated by filtration.	• When left to settle the insoluble particles separate from the liquid. • It forms a non-homogenous mixture. • Its parts can be separated by filtration

Common Errors

- A suspension is a saturated solution with excess solute.

  This is inaccurate as suspensions are not solutions as the fine-particled solid inside does not dissolve so it is not a solute and no solution is formed.

Step II Be the Teacher

This question is followed by three model answers.

One of these answers is a Grade A answer (above 80% correct), another a Grade C answer (around 50% correct). The third answer could be any grade (A to E).

Mark all three answers giving an appropriate grade with reasoning.

Question

When making a solution state three ways you could speed up the dissolving process. Identify the process that could be used to obtain the dissolved solute back from the solution? [4 marks]

Answer 1

Solutions can be made quicker by stirring more vigorously and heating the liquid doing the dissolving. Also if you ground up what you were dissolving the substance would dissolve more easily.

The dissolve substance can be obtained by evaporation of the solution.

Mark		Grade	

Reasoning: ....

....

The following would speed up dissolving:

1. Raising the temperature of the solvent.
2. The smaller the size of the solute particle the faster dissolve.
3. Stirring the solution a lot.

Distilling the solution would separate the dissolved solute from the solvent

Mark		Grade	

Reasoning: ....

....

Stirring and heating will speed up the dissolving. Also if you dissolve in a small beaker the solid will come into contact with the solvent more easily and will dissolve faster. Filtering the solution will help to get the solid back.

Mark		Grade	

Reasoning: ....

....

Actual Mark and Grade for Question

Solutions can be made quicker by stirring more vigorously and heating the liquid doing the dissolving. Also if you ground up what you were dissolving the substance would dissolve more easily.

The dissolve substance can be obtained by evaporation of the solution.

Mark	4	Grade	A

Reasoning: 3 marks for speeding up the dissolving (rate of stirring/higher temperature/increasing the surface area of dissolving substance).

The fourth mark is for obtaining the dissolved solid back, either by evaporation or distillation.

The following would speed up dissolving:

1 Raising the temperature of the solvent. ✓

2. The smaller the size of the solute particle the faster dissolve. ✓

3. Stirring the solution a lot. ✓

Distilling the solution would separate the dissolved solute from the solvent ✓

| Mark | 4 | Grade | A |

Reasoning: 3 marks for speeding up the dissolving (rate of stirring/higher temperature/increasing the surface area of dissolving substance).

The fourth mark is for obtaining the dissolved solid back, either by evaporation or distillation.

Stirring and heating ✓ ✓ will speed up the dissolving. Also if you dissolve in a small beaker the solid will come into contact with the solvent more easily and will dissolve faster. Filtering the solution will help to get the solid back.

| Mark | 2 | Grade | C |

Reasoning: Two marks for stirring and heating. No mark for dissolving in a smaller beaker.

Filtering only removes insoluble substances and does not separate the solid from a solution.

Step III Test Yourself

1. Identify two differences between a solution and a suspension.

    1. ....

    2. ....   [2]

2. The solubility of a substance (solute) is the amount of that substance which dissolves in 100 cm³ of water at a particular temperature.

Using only the apparatus shown below outline the stages involved for an experiment to measure the solubility of common salt (sodium chloride) at room temperature.

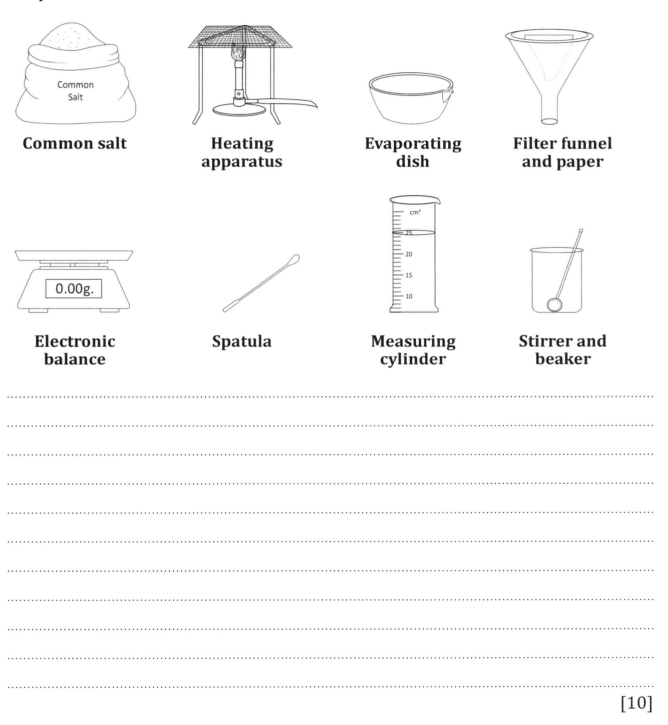

| **Common salt** | **Heating apparatus** | **Evaporating dish** | **Filter funnel and paper** |

| **Electronic balance** | **Spatula** | **Measuring cylinder** | **Stirrer and beaker** |

....

....

....

....

....

....

....

....

....

....

[10]

MODEL ANSWERS

1. Parts of a suspension can be separated by filtration but a solution cannot. [1]

   Suspension cloudy but solution clear [1]

   allow: suspension not the same throughout but solution is, suspension non-homogenous, suspension solid will settle out but solution will not

   ignore: suspension dirty, suspension heavier

2. Weigh empty evaporating dish. [1]

   Pour 25 cm^3 of water into beaker. [1]

   Add common salt with spatula to water and stir. [1]

   Add more salt until no more dissolves. [1]

   Weigh evaporating dish. [1]

   Filter salt solution into evaporating dish (previously weighed). [1]

   Slowly evaporate solution to dryness (avoid salt from spitting out) [1]

   Reweigh cooled evaporating dish and salt. [1]

   Find mass of salt dissolved by subtracting mass of empty evaporating dish. [1]

   The solubility of salt is this mass x 4 (as salt dissolved in 100 cm^3) [1]

   allow: alternative order of these ten marking points is allowed

   Total 20 marks

Separation Techniques

A. Filtration, Evaporation and Distillation

B. Magnetic Separation and Chromatography

C. Desalination and Reverse Osmosis

A. Filtration, Evaporation and Distillation

Step I Key Knowledge

- **Filtration** is used to **separate a mixture of a liquid and an insoluble solid**. For example, it can be used to separate a mixture of sand and water.

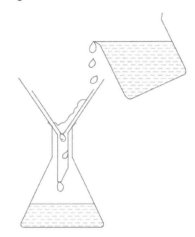

- The mixture is poured through a filter funnel which is lined with filter paper. The filter paper traps the insoluble substance (sand). This is called the **residue**. The liquid (water) passes through the filter paper and is collected in a beaker as the **filtrate**.

- **Evaporation** is used to **separate a mixture containing a soluble solid**. For example, separating salt from salt water.

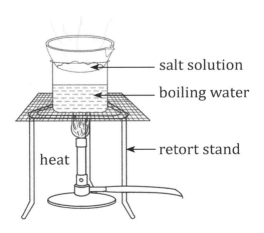

- The mixture to be evaporated is placed in the **evaporating dish**. This is heated gently using a **water bath** which prevents the solid salt from 'spitting out' from the dish. When all the water has evaporated and changed to steam, the **solid salt** will be left in the evaporating dish as the **residue**.

Common Errors

- Evaporation only occurs when a liquid boils.

  This is not true as evaporation occurs on the surface of any liquid. The liquid does not have to boil but the warmer a liquid is the greater the rate of evaporation.

- **Distillation** is used to **obtain a pure liquid from a solution,** such as separating pure water from seawater.

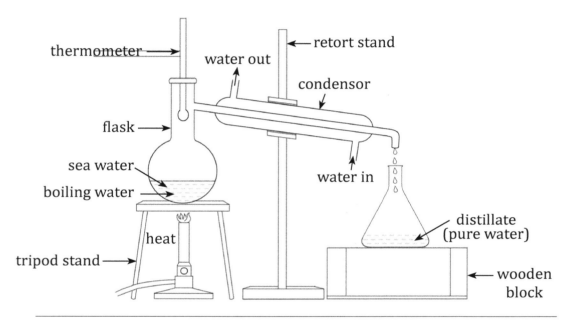

- Seawater is placed in the distilling flask. The porcelain chips in the flask ensure smooth boiling. On boiling, steam rises and goes into the **condenser**, where it is cooled by the cold-water jacket. The condensed water is the distillate and this drips into the conical flask where it collects as pure water. All the other substances present in the seawater remain in the distilling flask.

Step II Be the Teacher

This question is followed by three model answers.

One of these answers is a Grade A answer (above 80% correct), another a Grade C answer (around 50% correct). The third answer could be any grade (A to E).

Mark all three answers giving an appropriate grade with reasoning.

Question 1

Draw a *fully labelled* diagram of a distillation apparatus to obtain pure water from sea water. [6 marks]

Answer 1

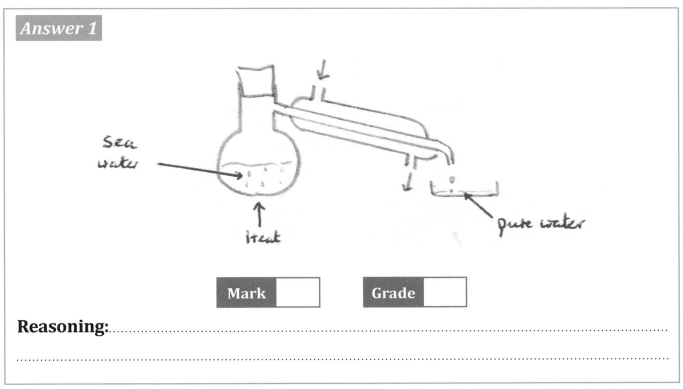

Mark		Grade	

Reasoning: ....
....

Answer 2

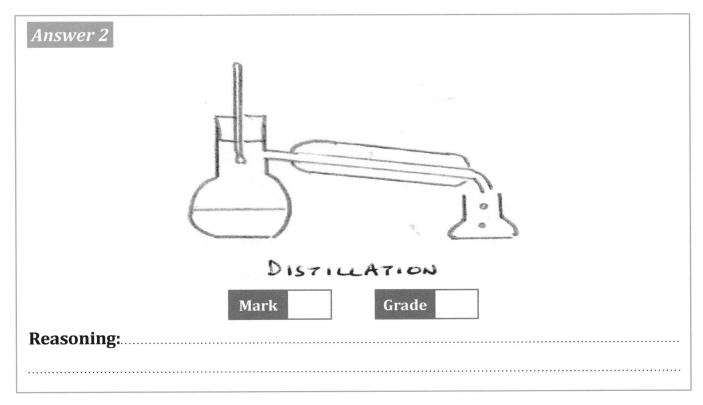

DISTILLATION

Mark		Grade	

Reasoning: ....
....

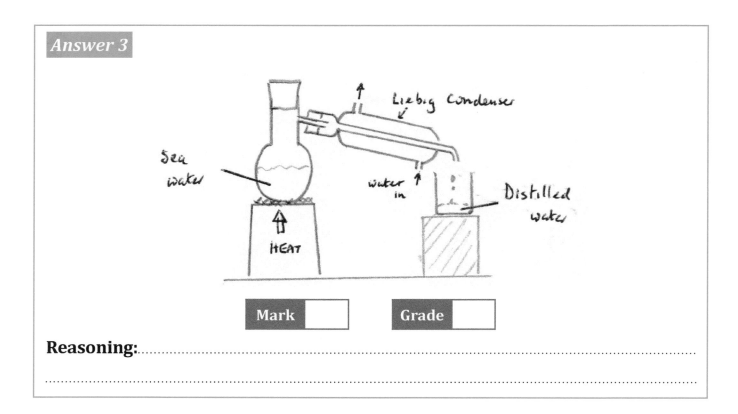

Mark ___   Grade ___

Reasoning:..
....

Actual Mark and Grade for Question

Answer 1

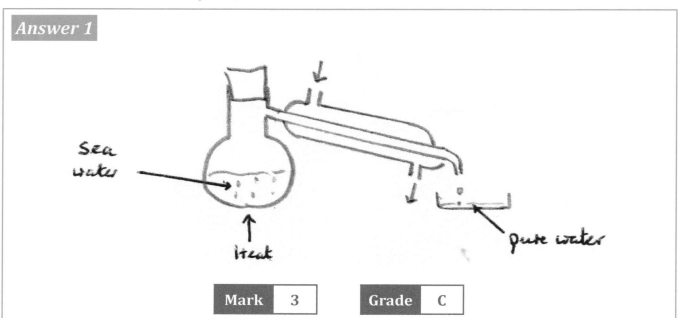

Mark 3   Grade C

Reasoning: The apparatus would work and sea water would be distilled by this apparatus.

However three marking points were lost for the following reasons:

* No thermometer shown in apparatus.

- Tube leading from round-bottomed flask should not be continuous as it passes through the condenser.

- Cold water should enter at the bottom of the condenser and leave from the top of the condenser. The condenser is not labelled.

Answer 2

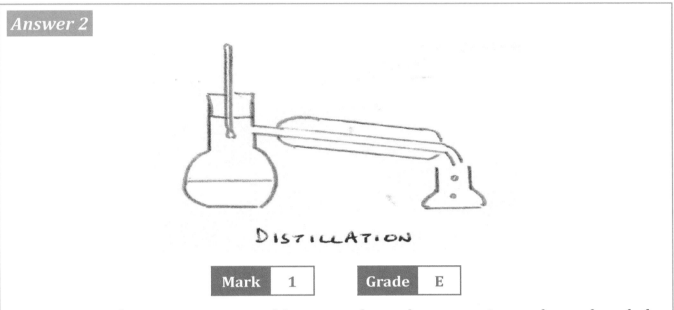

DISTILLATION

Mark	1		Grade	E

Reasoning: This apparatus would not work as the water is not heated and the condenser does not work. Also none of the parts of the apparatus are labelled.

However one mark was scored for putting the thermometer in the correct position to record the temperature of the vapour given off.

Answer 3

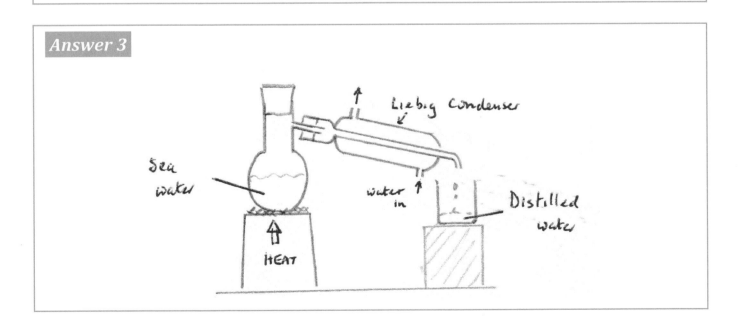

Reasoning: A good accurately labelled diagram of distillation. Pure distilled water could be collected using this apparatus. Cold water is shown entering at the bottom and leaving the top of the condenser.

One mark was deducted for not showing a thermometer in the round-bottomed flask to record the temperature of the vapour being distilled.

Question 2

A garden centre sells lawn sand which is a mixture of sand and a water-soluble fertiliser. Describe how you could separate this mixture in the laboratory. [6 marks]

Answer 1

First add water to the mixture and stir. The fertiliser will dissolve up while the sand will not. Pour the mixture through a filter funnel to remove the sand. Collect the clear water that passes through in an evaporating basin. Then heat the basin to evaporate the water so the fertiliser remains behind in the basin.

Mark		Grade	

Reasoning: ....
....
....

Answer 2

Add water to the mixture. The sand will sink to the bottom. The fertiliser will disappear as it dissolves. Carefully pour off the water from the sand. Then heat up the water so the fertiliser remains.

Mark		Grade	

Reasoning: ....
....
....

Answer 3

Add water to the mixture and shake to make sure it is all mixed together. Pour the shaken mixture through a filter funnel with filter paper inside. The sand will become trapped. Collect the clear water underneath and pour into a distillation apparatus. Distil off the water to leave the fertiliser behind.

Mark		Grade	

Reasoning: ....

....

....

....

Actual Mark and Grade for Question 2

Answer 1

First add water to the mixture and stir. The fertiliser will dissolve up while the sand will not. Pour the mixture through a filter funnel to remove the sand. Collect the clear water that passes through in an evaporating basin. Then heat the basin to evaporate the water so the fertiliser remains behind in the basin.

Mark	6	Grade	A

Reasoning: The description includes all six marking points.

The six marking points are as follows:

- Add water
- Stir (so the fertiliser dissolves)
- Sand will not dissolve/ only the fertiliser dissolves
- Filter to remove the sand / Accept decantation to separate sand
- Collect the clear liquid/solution
- Evaporate /Distil clear liquid to obtain the fertiliser

Answer 2

Add water to the mixture. The sand will sink to the bottom. The fertiliser will disappear as it dissolves. Carefully pour off the water from the sand. Then heat up the water so the fertiliser remains.

Mark	3		Grade	C

Reasoning: The description include three marking points:

- Adding water to mixture
- Sand sinking (not dissolving)
- Decantation...carefully pouring off water from sand.

Answer 3

Add water to the mixture and shake to make sure it is all mixed together. Pour the shaken mixture through a filter funnel with filter paper inside. The sand will become trapped. Collect the clear water underneath and pour into a distillation apparatus. Distil off the water to leave the fertiliser behind.

Mark	6		Grade	A

Reasoning: The description includes all six marking points.

- Add water
- Shake (so the fertiliser dissolves)
- Sand will not dissolve/ only the fertiliser dissolves
- Filter to remove the sand / Accept decantation to separate sand
- Collect the clear liquid/solution
- Evaporate /Distil clear liquid to obtain the fertiliser

Step III Be the Teacher

1. Complete the table by identifying the residue and filtrate of each of these mixtures after adding water, stirring and filtering the mixture.

Mixture	Residue	Filtrate
Sand and sugar		
Salt and sulfur		
Chalk and copper sulfate		

[6]

2. A substance X is soluble in alcohol but is insoluble in water. Another substance Y is soluble in water but insoluble in alcohol. Finally a third substance Z is soluble in both alcohol and water.

Using this information explain how would you obtain the following:

(a) X from a mixture of X and Y.

....

.... [2]

(b) Y from a mixture of X and Y.

....

.... [2]

(c) Z from a mixture of Y and Z.

....

....

.... [4]

MODEL ANSWERS

1.

Mixture	Residue		Filtrate	
Sand and sugar	Sand	[1]	Sugar solution	[1]
Salt and sulfur	Sulfur	[1]	Salt water	[1]
Chalk and copper sulfate	Chalk	[1]	Copper sulfate solution	[1]

ignore: do not accept filtrate unless indicate solution. For example salt as filtrate does not score.

2. (a) Add water to mixture (X and Y) and stir. [1] X not dissolve so separate by filtration. [1]
   allow: adding water to mixture

   (b) Add alcohol to mixture (X and Y) and stir. [1] Y not dissolve so separate by filtration. [1]
   allow: adding alcohol to mixture

   (c) Add alcohol to mixture (Y and Z) and stir. [1] Y does not dissolve. [1] Filter out Y and collect solution. [1] Evaporate solution to obtain Z. [1]
   allow: adding alcohol to mixture

Total 14 marks

B. Magnetic Separation and Chromatography

Step I Key Knowledge

- **Magnetic attraction** can be used to separate magnetic material from that which is not affected by a **magnetic force**. Magnetic material usually contains metals like **iron** or **cobalt** or **nickel**, or their alloys like **steel**.

> **Common Errors**
>
> - Magnetic separation can only be used to separate iron. This is not true as other metals like cobalt and nickel are also magnetic. Also magnetic separation can be used to separate alloys (mixtures of metals) which contain iron or cobalt or nickel. Steel and its various alloys can be magnetically separated.

- There are many types of chromatography. Paper chromatography is one type. **Paper chromatography** is normally used to **separate coloured components in mixtures**. Only a small amount of the mixture is needed.

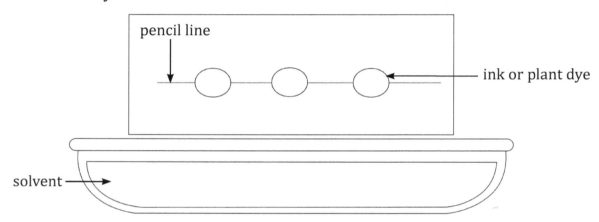

- Paper chromatography makes use of the fact that some coloured components dissolve in a liquid (called the solvent) better than others. Accordingly, they will be carried further up the chromatography paper by the liquid. Different **solvents** can be used to spread out these coloured components.

- Chromatographic separation can be very sensitive, separating minute quantities of different chemicals. It is used in detecting colourings used in foods/sweets. Also medical analysis of blood and urine and detecting illegal drugs used by athletes.

Step II Be the Teacher

This question is followed by three model answers.

One of these answers is a Grade A answer (above 80% correct), another a Grade C answer (around 50% correct). The third answer could be any grade (A to E).

Mark all three answers giving an appropriate grade with reasoning.

(a) **Explain how paper chromatography can be used to identify the various dyes in ink.** [4 marks]

(b) **Name two other uses of chromatography.** [2 marks]

Answer 1

(a) Spot the possible dyes the ink could contain on a sheet of chromatography paper. Place a spot of the ink in question to the side of these dyes. Dip the sheet in a solvent and leave for a while. All the dyes and ink will spread upwards. Whatever dyes the ink contains will be at the same level so you can work out which dyes it contains.

(b) Analysing colourings added to food, blood samples

Mark		Grade	

Reasoning: ....
....

Answer 2

(a) Set up a chromatography experiment as shown in the diagram.

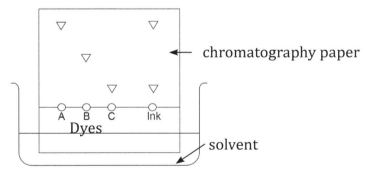

From the chromatogram you can see the ink contains dyes A and C but not B

(b) 1. In sport for testing for illegal drugs

   2. For police testing blood samples at crime scene

Mark		Grade	

Reasoning: ....
....

(a) Chromatography can be used to find the dyes in ink by spreading the dyes up a sheet of filter paper using a solvent. Some dyes will spread further up than others as they dissolve better.

(b) Doctors and police use chromatography.

| Mark | | Grade | |

Reasoning:...
....
....
....
....
....

Actual Mark and Grade for Question

Answer 1

(a) Spot the possible dyes the ink could contain on a sheet of chromatography paper. Place a spot of the ink in question to the side of these dyes. Dip the sheet in a solvent and leave for a while. All the dyes and ink will spread upwards. Whatever dyes the ink contains will be at the same level so you can work out which dyes it contains.

(b) Analysing colourings added to food, blood samples

| Mark | 6 | Grade | A |

Reasoning: (a) All four marking points were scored. The four marking points are as follows:

- Spotting chromatography paper with dyes and ink
- Dipping paper in solvent
- Dyes spreading to different heights
- Identifying dyes at the same level

(b) Both uses of chromatography are acceptable.

(a) Set up a chromatography experiment as shown in the diagram.

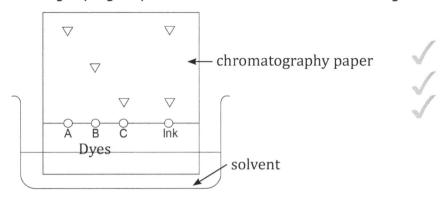

chromatography paper

A B C Ink

Dyes

solvent

From the chromatogram you can see the ink contains dyes A and C but not B

(b) 1. In sport for testing for illegal drugs

2. For police testing blood samples at crime scene

| Mark | 6 | Grade | A |

Reasoning: (a) The first three marks (spotting paper / solvent / spreading different heights) are scored from the diagram. Labelled diagrams are perfectly acceptable and it is often easier and quicker to draw a diagram than to try and explain in words. The fourth mark is also scored as concluded dye contains A and C from diagram.

(b) Both uses of chromatography are acceptable.

(a) Chromatography can be used to find the dyes in ink by spreading the dyes up a sheet of filter paper using a solvent. Some dyes will spread further up than others as they dissolve better.

(b) Doctors and police use chromatography.

| Mark | 3 | Grade | C |

Reasoning: (a) The first three marks (spotting paper / solvent / spreading different heights) are scored but not the fourth mark (same level identifies the dye present)

(b) No marks scored in uses as too vague.

Step III Test Yourself

1. State if these mixtures can be separated by magnetic separation. Explain your decision.

   (a) Mixture of steel and iron nails.

   ....

   .... [2]

   (b) Mixture of copper and brass pins.

   ....

   .... [2]

   (c) Mixture of copper and iron tacks.

   ....

   .... [2]

2. Consider the chromatogram shown below which is used to identify the food colourings in a particular sweet.

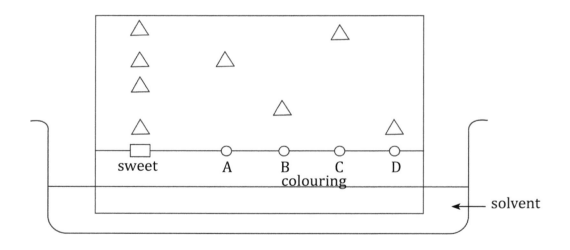

   (a) Explain why the solvent level should start below the spots of colourings and the sweet colour.

   .... [1]

   (b) Identify which colourings the sweet contains?

   .... [2]

(c) (i) Deduce if all the colourings used is this sweet are identified.

.... [1]

   (ii) Explain why it is important to identify all food additives and colourings used in making sweets.

....

.... [1]

MODEL ANSWERS

1. (a) Cannot be separated. [1] Both metals (steel and iron) are magnetic. [1]
   (b) Cannot be separated. [1] Both metals (copper and brass) are non-magnetic. [1]
   (c) Can be separated. [1] Iron is magnetic so will be attracted to the magnet. [1]
   allow: copper is not magnetic so will not be attracted to the magnet

2. (a) Prevent colourings from dissolving directly in the solvent. [1]
   (b) Sweet contains colourings A, C and D. [2]

      ignore: if only one colouring identified does not score, if four colourings identified scores 1 mark

   (c) (i) No because one colouring was not identified. [1]
          allow: no for the mark

      (ii) Some unapproved food colourings may have harmful effects on the human body. [1] or Makes sweets safe to eat. [1]
          allow: some food colourings may be poisonous

   Total 12 marks

C. Desalination and Reverse Osmosis

Step I Key Knowledge

- **Reverse osmosis** is a separation technique which is used to obtain fresh drinking water from seawater. This is called **desalination**.

- In osmosis, water passes through a **partially permeable membrane,** but the dissolved salts do not. However, if seawater is put under high pressure (about 25 atmospheres), water can be forced to travel through the partially permeable membrane, from the seawater side to the pure water side. The partially permeable membrane removes all traces of bacteria, viruses, chemicals and dissolved minerals.

- **Reverse osmosis** along **with filtration** is also used in **sewage plants** to purify water before discharging the water back into the rivers or sea.

Common Errors

- During reverse osmosis of sea water the salt instead of the water travels across the partially permeable membrane.

  This is untrue as it is still water moving across the partially permeable membrane but in the direction of low to high concentration, which is the reverse of normal osmosis.

Step II Be the Teacher

This question is followed by three model answers.

One of these answers is a Grade A answer (above 80% correct), another a Grade C answer (around 50% correct). The third answer could be any grade (A to E).

Mark all three answers giving an appropriate grade with reasoning.

Question

Explain how the technique of reverse osmosis is used to obtain fresh drinking water from sea water. [4 marks]

Answer 1

Reverse osmosis is movement of water only through a semi-permeable membrane from high concentration (sea water) to low concentration pure water). This occurs as sea water is put under high pressure. This way fresh drinking water is obtained from sea water.

Mark [ ]   Grade [ ]

Reasoning:..

....

....

....

The technique of reverse osmosis is used to obtain fresh drinking water from sea water as there is lots of sea water and people need fresh drinking water to stay alive. The technique is used in water plants in Singapore.

Mark		Grade	

Reasoning: ....
....
....

In reverse osmosis high pressure (about 25 atmospheres) pushes water across a partially permeable membrane. This is how you obtain fresh drinking water from sea water.

Mark		Grade	

Reasoning: ....
....
....

Actual Mark and Grade for Question 1

Reverse osmosis is movement of water only through a semi-permeable membrane from high concentration (sea water) to low concentration (pure water). This occurs as sea water is put under high pressure. This way fresh drinking water is obtained from sea water.

Mark	4	Grade	A

Reasoning: All four marks are scored for the following marking points:

- need semi-permeable (partially permeable) membrane
- high pressure on sea water
- from high concentration / sea water
- to low concentration / pure water

Answer 2

The technique of reverse osmosis is used to obtain fresh drinking water from sea water as there is lots of sea water and people need fresh drinking water to stay alive. The technique is used in water plants in Singapore.

| Mark | 0 | Grade | E |

Reasoning: No marks were scored as none of the marking points were mentioned.

The candidate has repeated the question which scores no marks. Also there are general points about importance of reverse osmosis but the question asked 'how reverse osmosis is used to obtain drinking water from sea water'. It is important to carefully read the question so you focus on what the examiner is asking.

Answer 3

In reverse osmosis high pressure (about 25 atmospheres) pushes water across a partially permeable membrane. This is how you obtain fresh drinking water from sea water.

| Mark | 2 | Grade | C |

Reasoning: Two marks for 'high pressure' and 'partially permeable membrane'.

Missing were the following marking points:

- from high concentration / sea water
- to low concentration / pure water

Step III Test Yourself

1. (a) Explain what is meant by desalination.

    ....

    ....

    .... [2]

(b) On some large passenger liners they obtain the drinking water used from the surrounding sea water using an apparatus shown below.

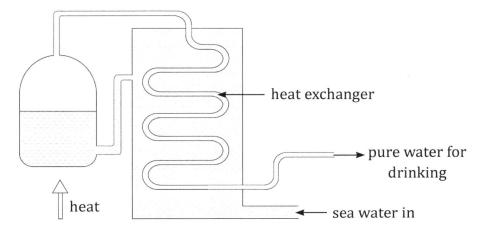

Explain how the apparatus works.

....

....

....

.... [4]

2. Explain the difference between osmosis and reverse osmosis.

....

....

.... [4]

$$\boxed{\text{MODEL ANSWERS}}$$

1. (a) Desalination is the removal of salt [1] (from seawater or other salty water) to make drinking water. [1]

   (b) Sea water is heated. [1]   Only pure water evaporates [1]. The steam passes into the heat exchanger where it is cooled down by the surrounding cold sea water. [1] The steam condenses and forms pure drinking water. [1]

2. Osmosis is the passage of water [1] from a less concentrated solution to a more concentrated solution [1] through a semi-permeable membrane.

   Reverse osmosis is the passage of water from a more concentrated solution to a less concentrated solution [1] (through a semi-permeable membrane). This is achieved by having high pressure on the more concentrated solution. [1] **ignore:** explanations of reverse osmosis as 'osmosis going backwards'

   Total 10 marks

Diversity of Living Things

A. Biodiversity of Life
B. Simple Living Organisms like Bacteria
C. Plant and Animal Kingdom
D. Dichotomous Keys to Identify Living Organisms

A. Biodiversity of Life

Step I Key Knowledge

- **Biodiversity** is a measure of the **total number of different living plants and animals** in an area.

- **Similar groups** of animals or plants are called **species**. Members of a species may breed with one another. Closely related species are called a genus (plural: genera) and all genera are grouped into **families**.

- Biodiversity is important because **we obtain many different things from plants and animals**. These include foods, medicines and many other raw materials like fibres for clothing (silk, cotton).

- **Biodiverse areas** are also much better at **recovering from natural disasters** like floods or tsunamis. The wide range of living organisms ensures quicker recovery.

- Within **biodiverse areas** it is also **less likely that a particular animal or plant will die out**. This is because the food webs within such areas are more complicated. Therefore if one food source disappears there is more likely to be an alternative available. Biodiversity helps to stabilise natural systems.

Common Errors

- Biodiversity indicates that an animal or plant is spread over a wide range of different habitats.

This is untrue. Biodiversity is a measure of the total number of **different** plants and animals in a particular area.

Step II Be the Teacher

This question is followed by three model answers.

One of these answers is a Grade A answer (above 80% correct), another a Grade C answer (around 50% correct). The third answer could be any grade (A to E).

Mark all three answers giving an appropriate grade with reasoning.

Question

Explain what is meant by the term biodiversity and state two examples of its importance. [4 marks]

Answer 1

Biodiversity is the ability of a living organism to survive. Examples are organisms using camouflage or standing very still so they cannot be seen.

Mark [　] Grade [　]

Reasoning: ....
....
....

Answer 2

Biodiversity is all the different plants and animals in a particular environment. It's important as it makes it more interesting for scientists to study the natural world if there are lots of different plants and animals.

Mark [　] Grade [　]

Reasoning: ....
....
....

Answer 3

Biodiversity is the total number of different plants and animals in an area. It is important as people may get different materials from living things. Also living things can survive better from a natural disaster in a biodiverse situation.

Mark [　] Grade [　]

Reasoning: ....
....
....

Actual Mark and Grade for Question

Answer 1

Biodiversity is the ability of a living organism to survive. Examples are organisms using camouflage or standing very still so they cannot be seen.

Mark 0   Grade E

Reasoning: No marks scored.

Biodiversity is a measure of the total number of plants and animals in an area.

Biodiverse areas have the following advantages:

- plants and animals can recover better from natural disasters like flooding etc.
- less likely that a particular organism will die out as the more complicated food webs allow alternative foods.
- biodiverse areas provide lots of useful materials like medicines, crops, raw materials (silk, cotton etc.)

Answer 2

Biodiversity is all the different plants and animals in a particular environment. It's important as it makes it more interesting for scientists to study the natural world if there are lots of different plants and animals.

Mark 2   Grade C

Reasoning: Two marks are scored for a correct definition.

It is true that it makes it more interesting for scientists to study a biodiverse area but this would not be classed as an advantage...only to scientists! Advantages need to be more general. For example

- plants and animals can recover better from natural disasters like flooding etc.
- less likely that a particular organism will die out as the more complicated food webs allow alternative foods.
- biodiverse areas provide lots of useful materials like medicines, crops, raw materials (silk, cotton etc.)

Biodiversity is the total number of different plants and animals in an area. It is important as people get may different materials from living things. Also living things can survive better from a natural disaster in a biodiverse situation.

| Mark | 4 | | Grade | A |

Reasoning: All four marks are scored.

Two marks for the correct definition of biodiversity and two marks for the correct advantages of a biodiverse area.

Step III Test Yourself

1. Food webs indicate the biodiversity of a particular area. Consider this simple food web.

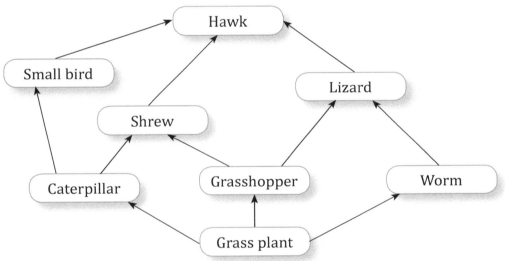

Identify the effects on the other animals in the food web that the following changes would have.

(a) The population of hawks decreased.

....

....

....

.... [4]

(b) The population of shrews increased.

....

....

.... [3]

(c) Global warming caused drought in the area so all the grass died off.

.... [1]

MODEL ANSWERS

1. (a) If population of hawks decreases there would be greater numbers of small birds, shrews and lizards. [1]

    This means there would be less caterpillars, grasshoppers and worms as more carnivores to eat them. [1]

    This would result in more grass as fewer herbivores. [1]

    Fourth mark for covering effect to all organisms in the food web. [1]

    (b) If population of shrews increased less caterpillars and grasshoppers. [1]

    This means there would be more grass as less herbivores. [1]

    Also if more shrews then more hawks as more food for the hawks. [1]

    (c) If all the grass dies off there would be lower populations of all organisms in the food web. [1]

Total 8 marks

B. **Simple Living Organisms like Bacteria**

Step I Key Knowledge

*   **Bacteria** (belonging to Kingdom Monera) are the **simplest living organisms** but they have a profound effect on mankind.

*   Their **ability to multiply** under the right conditions (moisture and warmth) is the bacteria's main strength

*   Sometimes the same bacteria can be **both helpful and harmful,** depending on what they are acting upon.

Activity of bacteria	Helpful	Harmful
Decomposing	Helps to break down dead and decaying matter, including sewage which prevents water pollution	Causes foodstuffs like meat and fish to go rotten and become inedible.

Activity of bacteria	Helpful	Harmful
In industry	Making of dairy products (butter, cheese, yoghurt) vinegar and biogas fuels.	Causes the souring of milk and wine
Affecting health	Producing antibiotics and hormones by genetic engineering.	Causes many different diseases in people. Also causes food poisoning.

Common Errors

- Freezing food kills any bacteria on the food.

  This is not so. However it does stop the bacteria from multiplying as they become dormant but on removing the food from the freezer the bacteria start to multiply up again. You should never put back food into the freezer once it has thawed.

Step II Be the Teacher

This question is followed by three model answers.

One of these answers is a Grade A answer (above 80% correct), another a Grade C answer (around 50% correct). The third answer could be any grade (A to E).

Mark all three answers giving an appropriate grade with reasoning.

Question

Identify two beneficial effects and two harmful effects of bacteria.   [4 marks]

Answer 1

Advantages of bacteria

1. Breakdown decaying matter like sewage.
2. Cause food to go off so you have to buy some more.

Disadvantages of bacteria

1. Multiply up very quickly
2. Cause different diseases

Mark [ ]   Grade [ ]

Reasoning:..
....

Answer 2

Harmful bacteria cause disease and make food go rotten. However some bacteria are useful as they help make cheese and can help in the digestion of food inside people.

Mark [ ]   **Grade** [ ]

Reasoning: ....
....
....

Answer 3

Good bacteria have no harmful effects whereas bad bacteria can cause disease and illness like coughs and stomach upsets.

Mark [ ]   **Grade** [ ]

Reasoning: ....
....
....

Actual Mark and Grade for Question

Answer 1

Advantages of bacteria

1. Breakdown decaying matter like sewage. ✓

2. Cause food to go off so you have to buy some more.

Disadvantages of bacteria

1. Multiply up very quickly

2. Cause different diseases ✓

Mark 2   **Grade** C

Reasoning: Only one advantage is correct (breaking down matter like sewage). Causing food to go off is a disadvantage of bacteria.

Only one disadvantage is correct (cause disease). Bacteria do multiply up quickly but that can be an advantage. For example if they are useful bacteria breaking down sewage then you want them to multiply quickly

Answer 2

Harmful bacteria cause disease and make food go rotten. However some bacteria are useful as they help make cheese and can help in the digestion of food inside people.

Mark	4		Grade	A

Reasoning: Two correct disadvantages and two correct advantages scores the full four marks.

Answer 3

Good bacteria have no harmful effects whereas bad bacteria can cause disease and illness like coughs, infections and stomach upsets.

Mark	1		Grade	D

Reasoning: Good bacteria have no harmful effects is too vague to score any marks for advantages.

Bacteria cause disease scores only one mark even though there are three correct examples of bacterial disease.

Step III Test Yourself

1. (a) Identify three favourable conditions that would allow bacteria to multiply.

....

.... [3]

(b) Under favourable conditions bacteria can multiply so that one bacteria becomes two bacteria every half-hour.
How many would 1 000 bacteria become in 4 hours?

....

....

.... [3]

MODEL ANSWERS

1. Warmth [1] Moisture [1] Dark/little light [1]

    allow: damp, wet, water, no direct sunlight

    ignore: high temperature

2. 1 000 → 2 000 → 4 000 (1 hour) → 8 000 → 16 000 (2 hours) →
    32 000 → 64 000 (3 hours) → 128 0000 → 256 000 bacteria (4 hours) [3]

    allow: saying 256 000 with no calculation scores 3 marks

    answers between 250 000 – 260 000 scores 2 marks

    answers between 200 000 – 300 000 scores 1 mark

    Total 6 marks

C. Plant Kingdom and Animal Kingdom

Step I Key Knowledge

• Living organisms can broadly be classified into five groups called **five kingdoms**.

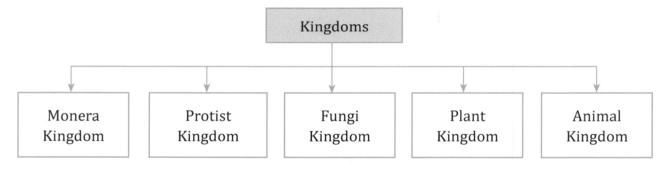

• The **animal and plant kingdoms** are the biggest groups and we shall focus on these main subdivisions of living things.

• Plants can be divided into two main groups: **seed** and **seedless** plants.

Type of seed plant	Characteristics
Flowering (hibiscus, lily, grass etc.)	• They produce flowers • Their seeds are found inside the fruit
Non-flowering (juniper, pine, cycad etc.)	• Produce cones instead of flowers • Their seed are inside the cone.

- Seedless plants fall into three main groups: **algae, fungi** and **ferns**.

Type of seedless plant	Characteristics
Algae and **moss** (spirogyra, seaweed etc.)	• Simple plants that do not have roots stems or leaves • Live in water or damp places • They contain green chlorophyll
Fungi (mushrooms, toadstools breadmould etc.)	• Do not have chlorophyll and cannot make their own food. • Reproduce by tiny spores.
Fern (bracken, bird's nest)	• They reproduce from spores on the underneath of their leaves. • Contain green chlorophyll

- Animals can be divided into those with backbones **(vertebrates)** and those without backbones **(invertebrates)**.
- **Vertebrates** can be divided into five groups: **fish, amphibians, reptiles, birds** and **mammals.**

Type of vertebrate	Characteristics
Fish (eel, trout, shark, seahorse etc.)	• Cold blooded and live in water. • Bodies covered with slimy scales. • Have gills for breathing. • Have fins for swimming.
Amphibians (frog, toad, newt, salamander etc.)	• Cold blooded • Have moist skin (no scales or hair). • Live on both land and water but always lay their eggs in water. • Have four legs.

Type of vertebrate	Characteristics
Reptile (snake, crocodile, tortoise, lizard etc.)	• Cold blooded • Have leathery skin covered in scales • Always lay their eggs on land • Eggs have soft shells
Birds (penguin, vulture, eagle etc.)	• Warm blooded • Bodies covered with feathers. • Have beaks and no teeth. • Lay eggs with hard shells.
Mammals (bat, dolphin, seal, whale, human being etc.)	• Warm blooded • Bodies covered with hair or fur. • Mothers produce milk for their babies.

• **Invertebrates** can be divided into two main groups: those **without legs** (worms and snails) and those **with jointed legs** (arthropods).

Type of invertebrate	Characteristics
Without legs	Two main group • **Worm-like** with segmented bodies like earthworm or leech • **Not worm-like** like snail, sea-anemone, starfish
With jointed legs (arthropods)	• Have exoskeleton • Main group are insects with three body sections (ants, bees, butterflies, flies, grasshoppers etc.) • Other group have more than three pairs of legs like spiders (4 pairs), crustacea (5 pairs), millipedes etc.

Common Errors

- Sharks and dolphins belong to the same group of animals.... not true. Sharks are cold-blooded and are fish. Dolphins are mammals as they suckle their young and are warm blooded.

- Salamanders and snakes belong to the same group of animals......not true. Salamanders are amphibians and lay their eggs in water but snakes are reptiles and lay their eggs on land.

- Bats and penguins belong to the same group of animals....not true. Bats are mammals as bodies covered with hair and they give milk to their young. Penguins are birds laying eggs and are covered with feathers.

Step II Be the Teacher

This question is followed by three model answers.

One of these answers is a Grade A answer (above 80% correct), another a Grade C answer (around 50% correct). The third answer could be any grade (A to E).

Mark all three answers giving an appropriate grade with reasoning.

Question

A turtle and a frog are both classified as cold-blooded vertebrate animals. However the frog is an amphibian and a turtle a reptile.

By considering their skin, eggs and habitat compare amphibian and reptile [6 marks]

Answer 1

Turtles lay eggs on land but live in the sea. Frogs lay eggs in water but live on the land. Both are cold-blooded vertebrates but have a skin which is porous to let warm air into the blood.

Mark		Grade	

Reasoning: ....
....
....
....

Answer 2

Frogs have a smooth moist skin with no scales but turtles have leathery rough skin with scales.

Frogs lay eggs in water. Turtles lay eggs on land.

Frogs live on both land and water but turtles live in the sea.

Mark		Grade	

Reasoning: ....

....

....

Answer 3

They both have backbones but as they are cold-blooded they both have to warm themselves in the Sun before they can become active. The skin of the frog warms up quicker than the skin of the turtle.

The turtle is nocturnal and lays its eggs at night. The frog lays its eggs during the day.

Mark		Grade	

Reasoning: ....

....

....

Actual Mark and Grade for Question

Answer 1

Turtles lay eggs on land but live in the sea. Frogs lay eggs in water but live on the land. Both are cold-blooded vertebrates but have a skin which is porous to let warm air into the blood.

Mark	3	Grade	C

Reasoning: Two marks for turtles laying eggs on land and frogs laying eggs on water.

One mark for turtles living in the sea (have flippers). However to score the habitat mark for the frog you need to emphasise that it lives on both land and water (amphibian).

No marks for skin as their skin does not let warm air pass through.

Answer 2

Frogs have a smooth moist skin with no scales but turtles have leathery rough skin with scales.

Frogs lay eggs in water. Turtles lay eggs on land.

Frogs live on both land and water but turtles live in the sea.

| Mark | 6 | Grade | A |

Reasoning: A commendable answer with all six marks scored.

Two marks for the correct difference in their skin. Two marks for turtle laying eggs on land and frog laying eggs in water. Two marks for turtle living in the sea whereas frog, as it is an amphibian, living on both land and water.

Answer 3

They both have backbones but as they are cold-blooded they have to warm themselves in the Sun before they can become active. The skin of the frog warms up quicker than the skin of the turtle.

The turtle is nocturnal and lays its eggs at night. The frog lays its eggs during the day.

| Mark | 0 | Grade | E |

Reasoning: The aim of the question was to distinguish between an amphibian and reptile animal, so confirming they have no backbone and are cold-blooded, scores no mark. Marks cannot be scored by repeating information given in the question.

The two points made about their skin and when they lay their eggs are wrong. Overall there are no marks scored.

Step III Test Yourself

1. Oscar and his friends were discussing classification of plants. Below are the six statements they made.

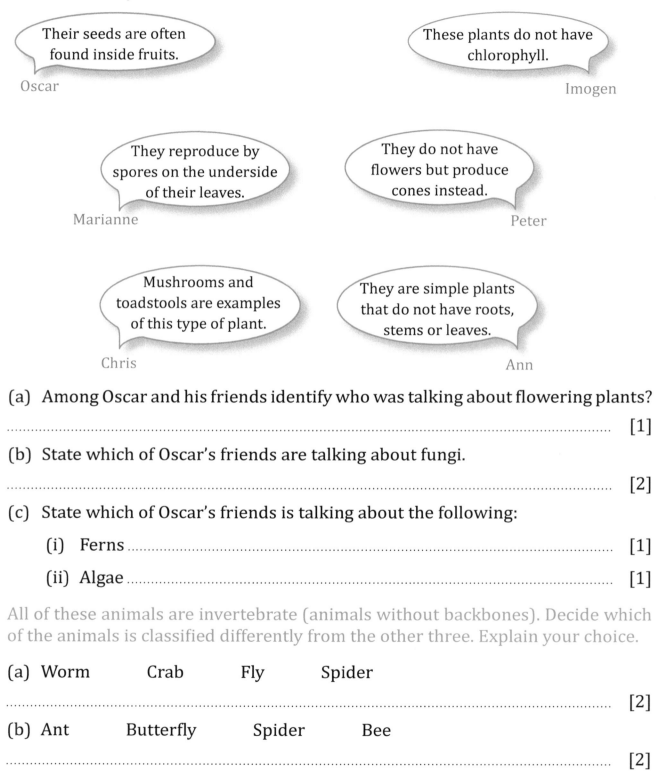

Their seeds are often found inside fruits.
Oscar

These plants do not have chlorophyll.
Imogen

They reproduce by spores on the underside of their leaves.
Marianne

They do not have flowers but produce cones instead.
Peter

Mushrooms and toadstools are examples of this type of plant.
Chris

They are simple plants that do not have roots, stems or leaves.
Ann

   (a) Among Oscar and his friends identify who was talking about flowering plants?

   .... [1]

   (b) State which of Oscar's friends are talking about fungi.

   .... [2]

   (c) State which of Oscar's friends is talking about the following:

   (i) Ferns .... [1]

   (ii) Algae .... [1]

2. All of these animals are invertebrate (animals without backbones). Decide which of the animals is classified differently from the other three. Explain your choice.

   (a) Worm   Crab   Fly   Spider

   .... [2]

   (b) Ant   Butterfly   Spider   Bee

   .... [2]

3. (a) Each of the five animals in the table belong to a **different** class of vertebrate (animals with backbones).

Complete the table to identify the class of vertebrate the animal belongs to.

Animal	Class of Vertebrate
Seal	
Salamander	
Tortoise	
Shark	
Penguin	

[5]

(b) (i) Which two of these vertebrate animals are warm-blooded?

....

.... [2]

(ii) Give one specific characteristic of each of the three remaining animals which identifies which class of vertebrate they belong to.

....

....

....

.... [3]

MODEL ANSWERS

1. (a) Oscar [1]
   (b) Imogen [1] Chris [1]
   (c) (i) Marianne [1]   (ii) Ann [1]

2. (a) Worm [1] has no legs [1]
   allow: others (crab, fly, spider) are arthropods
   (b) Spider [1] as others are insects [1]
   allow: spider has 8 legs, others (insects) have 6 legs

3. (a)

Animal	Class of Vertebrate	
Seal	Mammal	[1]
Salamander	Amphibian	[1]
Tortoise	Reptile	[1]
Shark	Fish	[1]
Penguin	Bird	[1]

(b) (i)   seal [1]   penguin [1]

(ii) salamander...accept live on land and water or moist skin or four legs   [1]
    ignore: cold-blooded

    tortoise...accept leathery skin or lay eggs on land or eggs have soft shells   [1]
    allow: scaly skin, scales
    ignore: cold-blooded

    shark....gills for breathing or fins for swimming or scales on body   [1]
    allow: gills, fins, scales
    ignore: cold-blooded

Total 19 marks

D. Dichotomous Keys

Step I Key Knowledge

- A **dichotomous key** shows how objects or organisms are grouped according to their common characteristics. To make a dichotomous key, we need to identify **similarities** and **differences** among objects.

- To make a dichotomous key of a group of objects or organisms, we should follow these steps:

    ➢ Step 1   Identify one main difference to divide the group into two.

    ➢ Step 2   Within the two main groups, identify another difference that can divide each into two subgroups.

    ➢ Step 3   Continue to identify differences that can split each small subgroup into two, until every group is left with just one member.

    ➢ Step 4   Draw up the key according to your classification.

Common Errors

- Using dichotomous keys you can identify similarities between objects.

  This is incorrect as you must identify a difference of one of the objects from the others. The question can then be asked to distinguish this object from the rest. The process is then repeated identifying a difference of one object from the other remaining objects.

Step II Be the Teacher

This question is followed by three model answers.

One of these answers is a Grade A answer (above 80% correct), another a Grade C answer (around 50% correct). The third answer could be any grade (A to E).

Mark all three answers giving an appropriate grade with reasoning.

Question

Draw a dichotomous key to distinguish these six shopping items.

green cabbage	washing-up liquid	red peppers
cheese	bar of soap	milk

Answer 1

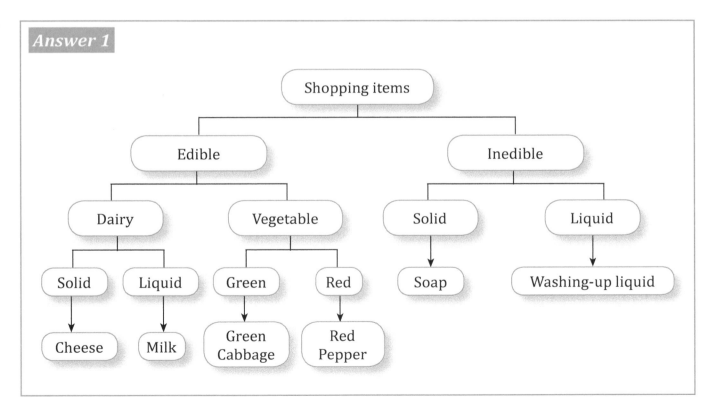

Mark [ ]   **Grade** [ ]

Reasoning: ....
....
....
....
....
....

Answer 2

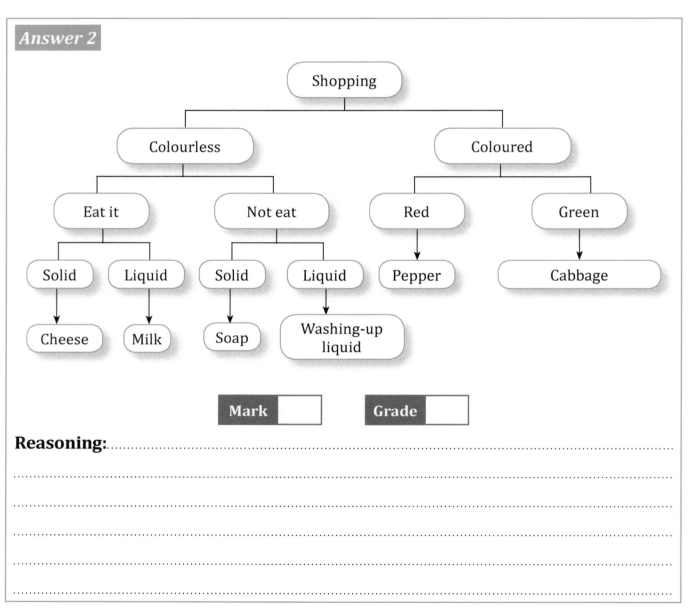

Mark [ ]   **Grade** [ ]

Reasoning: ....
....
....
....
....
....

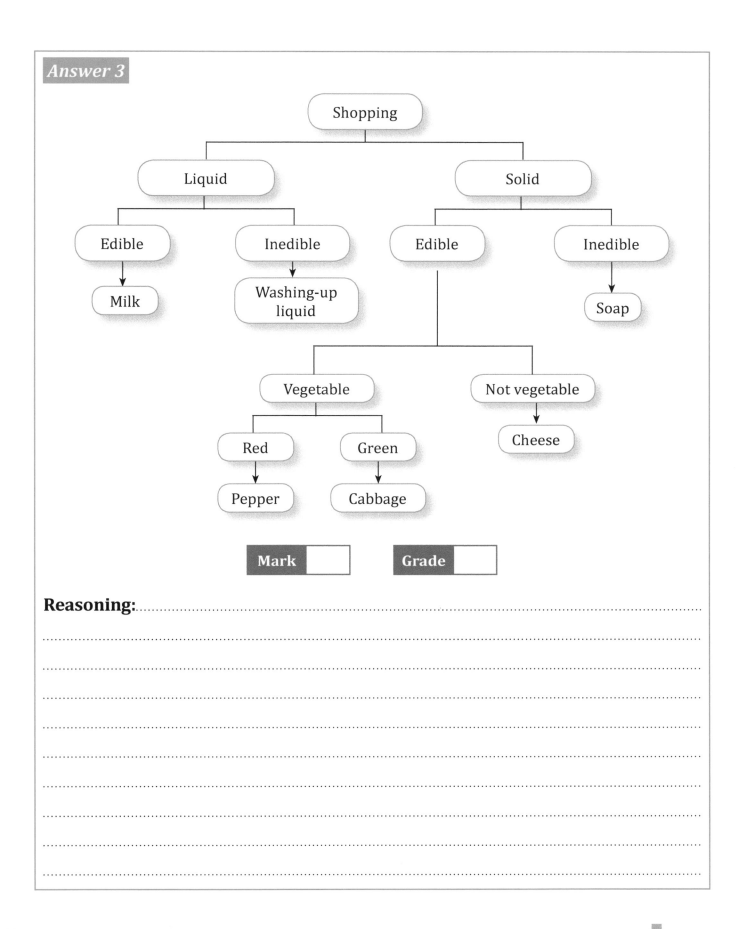

Answer 3

Shopping

- Liquid
  - Edible → Milk
  - Inedible → Washing-up liquid
- Solid
  - Edible
    - Vegetable
      - Red → Pepper
      - Green → Cabbage
    - Not vegetable → Cheese
  - Inedible → Soap

Mark [ ]   Grade [ ]

Reasoning: ....
....
....
....
....
....
....
....
....

Actual Mark and Grade for Question

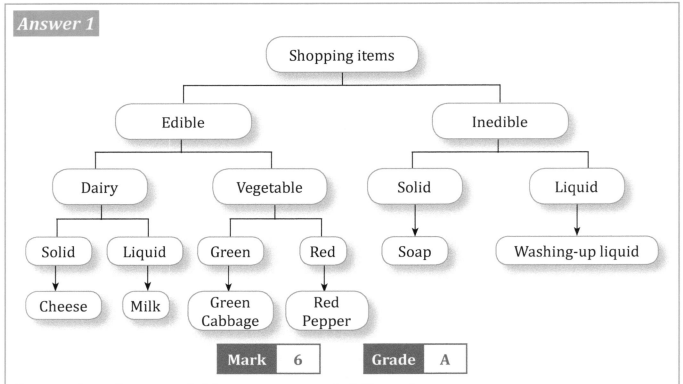

Answer 1

Mark 6   **Grade** A

Reasoning: Commendable answer worth full marks.

Student has identified a main difference between the six items (edible / inedible). Within these two main groups they have then identified another main difference. Then a further difference (solid / liquid or green / red) to correctly identify the four objects in one of the group

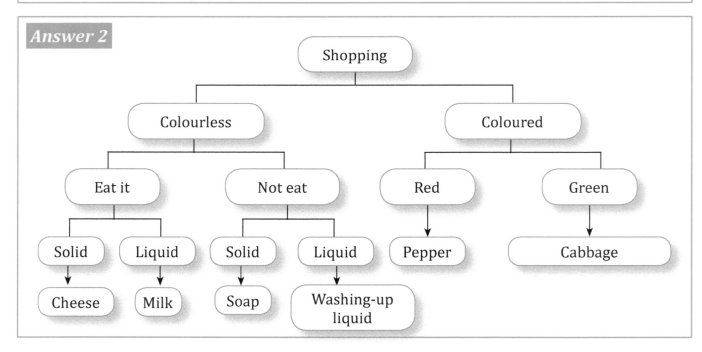

Answer 2

Mark	3		Grade	C

Reasoning: The initial main difference to divide the group of items into two is not accurate as cheese, milk, soap and washing-up liquid do have colour and are not colourless.

After this the dichotomous key works so student awarded 3 marks for their key.

Answer 3

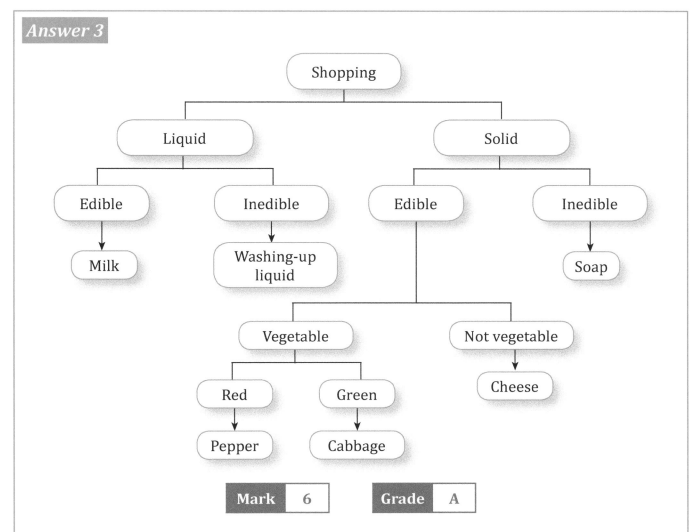

Mark	6		Grade	A

Reasoning: The dichotomous key works so is awarded full marks. There are often several different dichotomous keys which can be used to identify individual items in a group. What changes the key is the initial key question.

Step III Test Yourself

1. The following dichotomous key is used to identify vertebrate animals.

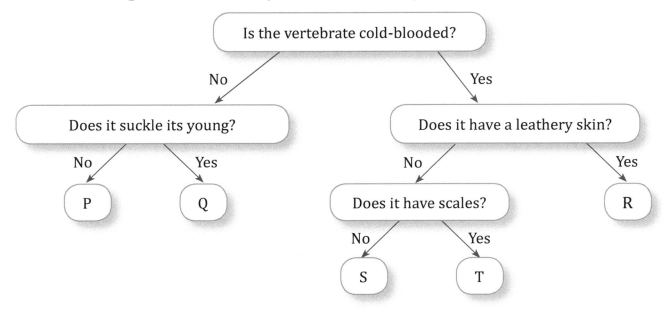

Name the five types of vertebrate in this dichotomous key.

P .... Q ....

R .... S ....

T .... [5]

2. The following dichotomous key can be used to identify arthropods
    (invertebrates with segmented bodies and legs).

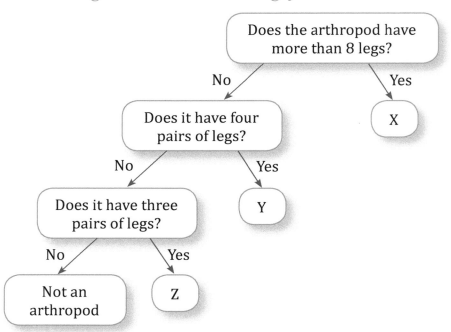

In which group X, Y or Z would you find the following arthropods:

(a) Spider .... (b) Millipede ....

(c) Butterfly .... (d) Bee ....

(e) Fly .... (f) Insect ....

(g) Centipede .... [7]

MODEL ANSWERS

1. P... Bird [1]   Q...Mammal [1]

   R...Reptile [1]   S....Amphibian [1]

   T...Fish [1]

2. (a) Y [1]   (b) X [1]   (c) Z [1]

   (d) Z [1]   (e) Z [1]   (f) Z [1]

   (g) X [1]

Cells – The Basic Units of Life

A. Different Parts of a Living Cell

Step I Key Knowledge

- **Cells** are the **basic building unit of all living organisms**. All organisms are made up of living cells.

- A typical cell contains four main parts: **nucleus**, **cytoplasm**, **cell membrane** and **vacuoles**. In addition, **plant cells** contain a **cell wall** and **chloroplasts**.

Part of cell	Features	Function
Nucleus	Contain chromosomes which contain the hereditary material of the cell.	Controls chemical reactions in cell and is responsible for cell reproduction.
Cytoplasm	Jelly-like substance that surrounds the nucleus.	Place where the chemical reactions of the cell take place.
Cell membrane	Partially permeable membrane around the cell.	Controls movement of substances in and out of the cell.
Vacuoles	Animal cells have many vacuoles but plant cells only one large vacuole.	Space for temporarily storing air, liquid and food particles.
Cell wall	Thick rigid layer around cell membrane.	Makes plant cells firm in shape.
Chloroplasts	Tiny discs containing green chlorophyll.	Chlorophyll traps the sunlight energy that the plant needs to make food.

Common Errors

- Cells are small, circular structures found in all living organisms…. not true.

  Cells are small but vary in size according to the job they perform. Their shape also varies according their function. Often animal cells are roundish but plant cells are normally rectangular as they are normally stationary inside the plant.

Step II Be the Teacher

This question is followed by three model answers.

One of these answers is a Grade A answer (above 80% correct), another a Grade C answer (around 50% correct). The third answer could be any grade (A to E).

Mark all three answers giving an appropriate grade with reasoning.

Question

Most cells cannot be seen by the naked eye. A microscope is used to see them. A student used a simple light microscope with an eyepiece magnification of 5x and an objective lens magnification of 30x.

(a) When the student looked at an onion cell using the microscope, it appeared 1.5 cm in diameter. Calculate the onion cell's actual diameter. [2 marks]

(b) The average size of an onion cell's nucleus is 0.01 mm. Calculate the size this nucleus would appear using this microscope with the same magnification. [2 marks]

Answer 1

(a) Overall magnification of microscope = $5 \times 30 = 150$x
So true diameter of cell = $1.5 / 150 = 0.01$ cm

(b) The nucleus would appear 150x times larger
So appear $150 \times 0.01 = 1.5$ cm (under microscope)

Mark		Grade	

Reasoning:..
....

Answer 2

(a) 0.1 mm   (b) 1.5 mm

Mark		Grade	

Reasoning:..
....
....

Answer 3

(a) The onion cell would appear much larger under the microscope so its true diameter is much smaller than 1.5 cm.

(b) The onion cell nucleus would appear 150x larger

$$= 150 \times 0.01 \text{ mm} = 1.5 \text{ mm}$$

Mark		Grade	

Reasoning:...
....

Actual Mark and Grade for Question

Answer 1

(a) Overall magnification of microscope = 5 x 30 = 150x
So true diameter of cell = 1.5 /150 = 0.01 cm ✓

(b) The nucleus would appear 150x times larger
So appear 150 × 0.01 = 1.5 cm (under microscope)

Mark	3	Grade	B

Reasoning: (a) Correct answer for 150x larger with correct units so scores both marks.

(b) Scores 1 mark as wrong units. Should be 1.5 mm (not cm).

Answer 2

(a) 0.1 mm ✓ (b) 1.5 mm ✓

Mark	4	Grade	A

Reasoning: Both answers are correct with correct units, so score 2 marks each.

A correct answer to a calculation with correct units will score full marks for the question. It is not necessary to show working, but it is highly advisable. Showing working allows you to score marks for correct sections in a calculation, even though you end up with an incorrect answer.

(a) The onion cell would appear much larger under the microscope so its true diameter is much smaller than 1.5 cm.

(b) The onion cell nucleus would appear 150x larger

= 150 × 0.01 mm = 1.5 mm ✓

| Mark | 2 | | Grade | C |

Reasoning: (a) No marks as no calculation of true size of onion cell.

(b) Correct calculation with correct units so scores two marks.

Step III Test Yourself

1. Sazali and his friends were discussing different parts of a cell. Below are the six statements each friend made.

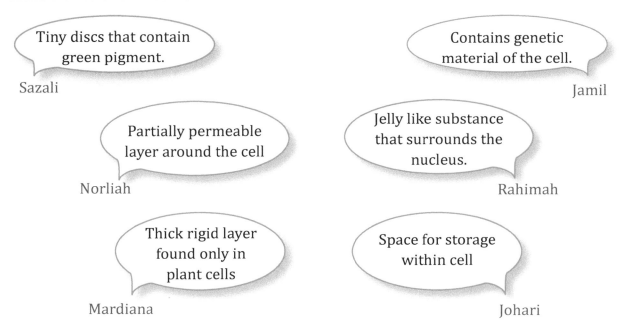

Tiny discs that contain green pigment.

Sazali

Contains genetic material of the cell.

Jamil

Partially permeable layer around the cell

Norliah

Jelly like substance that surrounds the nucleus.

Rahimah

Thick rigid layer found only in plant cells

Mardiana

Space for storage within cell

Johari

Identify the part of the cell each friend describes

Sazali .... 　　Jamil .... 　　Norliah ....

Rahimah .... 　　Mardiana .... 　　Johari .... 　　[6]

2. Consider these statements about the functions of different parts of a cell.

I. Acts as a chemical factory where the many chemical reactions take place.

II. Controls chemical reactions in the cell.

III. Controls movement of substances in and out of the cell.

IV. Traps sunlight that the plant needs to make food.

V. Temporarily contains air, liquid or food particles

VI. Supports and gives the plant cell its shape.

Identify the part of the cell that carries out these functions.

I ....   II ....   III ....

IV ....   V ....   VI ....   [6]

MODEL ANSWERS

1. Sazali... Chloroplasts [1] Jamil... Nucleus [1] Norliah... Cell membrane [1]

   Rahimah... Cytoplasm [1] Mardiana... Cell wall [1] Johari... Vacuole [1]

   allow: chromosome for nucleus

   ignore: chlorophyll for chloroplasts

2. I... Cytoplasm [1]   II... Nucleus [1]   III... Cell membrane [1]

   IV... Chlorophyll [1]   V... Vacuole [1]   VI... Cell wall [1]

   allow: chloroplast for chlorophyll

   Total 12 marks

B. Typical Plant and Animal Cells

Step I Key Knowledge

• There are important **differences between a plant and animal cell**.

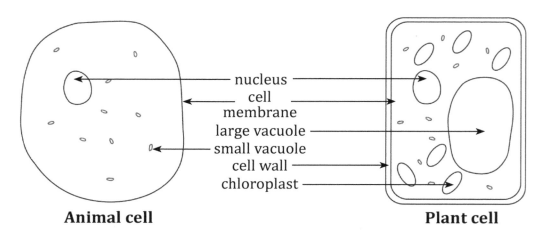

Animal cell   Plant cell

Animal cell	Plant cell
Has many small vacuoles.	Has one large vacuole containing cell sap.
Does not contain chloroplasts.	Contain chloroplasts with chlorophyll.
Does not have a cell wall.	Have cell wall to give plant cell its shape.
Most of the cell is filled with cytoplasm.	Has a thin lining of cytoplasm.

Common Errors

- Animal cells have a cell membrane but plant cells have a cell wall....not true.

  Animal cells have a cell membrane but plant cells have a cell membrane and a cell wall to give the plant cell a rigid structure.

Step II Be the Teacher

This question is followed by three model answers.

One of these answers is a Grade A answer (above 80% correct), another a Grade C answer (around 50% correct). The third answer could be any grade (A to E).

Mark all three answers giving an appropriate grade with reasoning.

Question

Explain how you would distinguish between plant and animal cells that were viewed under a microscope. [6 marks]

Answer 1

The differences you would see are shown in the table.

Animal Cell	Plant cell
Has cytoplasm	Does not have any cytoplasm
No chloroplasts	Chloroplasts for photosynthesis
Has cell membrane	Has cell wall

Mark [ ]   Grade [ ]

Reasoning:..
....
....

Plant cells have a rigid cell wall but animal cells do not. Plant cells have one large vacuole but animal cells have lots of smaller vacuoles. Also plant cells have chloroplasts full of chlorophyll. Animal cells do not photosynthesise so don't have chloroplasts.

Mark [   ]   Grade [   ]

Reasoning:...
....
....

Answer 3

Animal cells are a different shape to plant cells. They also have larger nuclei with a lot more chromosomes than plants. Animal cells also have nerve sensors but plant cells do not.

Mark [   ]   Grade [   ]

Reasoning:...
....
....

Actual Mark and Grade for Question 1

Answer 1

The differences you would see are shown in the table.

Animal Cell	Plant cell
Has cytoplasm	Does not have any cytoplasm
No chloroplasts	Chloroplasts for photosynthesis
Has cell membrane	Has cell wall

| Mark | 3 | | Grade | C |

Reasoning: It is a good idea when making a comparison to draw a table.

Three of the differences are accurate (presence of chloroplasts and cell wall only in plants).

However the other three points made in the table do not score. Plants and animal cells both contain cytoplasm (jelly-like substance around the nucleus). Also both animal and plant cells have cell membranes.

Answer 2

Plant cells have a rigid cell wall but animal cells do not. Plant cells have one large vacuole but animal cells have lots of smaller vacuoles. Also plant cells have chloroplasts full of chlorophyll. Animal cells do not photosynthesise so don't have chloroplasts.

| Mark | 6 | | Grade | A |

Reasoning: A commendable answer. All six marks are scored for correctly pointing out the presence of cell walls and chloroplasts only in plant cells and the difference in size of the vacuoles.

Answer 3

Animal cells are a different shape to plant cells. They also have much larger nuclei than plants. Animal cells also have nerve sensors but plant cells do not.

| Mark | 0 | | Grade | E |

Reasoning: No marks are scored as differences inaccurate or too vague.

Animal cells do have different shapes and sizes to plants but it is difficult to generalise. Also it is difficult to generalise about the size of the nuclei in plants and animals. Animal cells do not have nerve sensors. These nerve sensors are specialised cells in themselves.

Step III Test Yourself

1. The diagram shows a typical animal and plant cell.

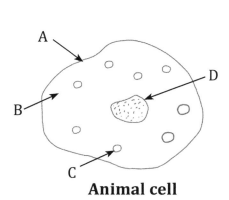

Animal cell

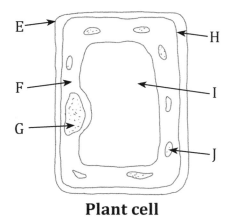

Plant cell

(a) (i) Identify the four labelled parts of the animal cell.

A ....   B ....

C ....   D ....   [4]

(ii) Identify the six labelled parts of the plant cell.

E ....   F ....

G ....   H ....

I ....   J ....   [6]

(b) With the help of these diagrams state three differences between an animal and plant cell.

1. ....

2. ....

3. ....   [3]

(c) Explain why animals are classified as consumers (eat other plants or animals for their food) but plants as producers (make their own food).

....

....   [2]

MODEL ANSWERS

1. (a) (i) A... Cell membrane [1] B... Cytoplasm [1] C... Vacuole [1]
       D... Nucleus [1]

   allow: nuclear wall for nucleus (D)

   (ii) E... Cell wall [1] F... Cytoplasm [1] G... Nucleus [1]

       H... Cell membrane [1] I... Vacuole [1] J... Chloroplast [1]

   allow: chromosome for nucleus (G)

   (b) Plant cells normally have one large vacuole, animal cells lots of vacuoles. [1]

   ignore: reference to only the plant or the animal cell. You need to compare both.

   Plants have chloroplasts, animal cells do not   [1]

   allow: chlorophyll for chloroplast

   ignore: reference to only the plant or the animal cell. You need to compare both.

   Plant cells have cell wall, animal cell does not   [1]

   ignore: reference to only the plant or the animal cell. You need to compare both.

   (c) Only plant cells contain chloroplasts [1] and therefore can photosynthesise [1] and make simple foods. They are therefore producers.

   allow: only plants have chlorophyll

   Total 15 marks

C. **Organisation of Cells into Tissues, Organs and Systems**

Step I Key Knowledge

- **Cells** come in many **different shapes** and **sizes**. Each type of cell has a special job to do.

- In a **multicellular organism**, cells performing specific tasks are grouped together into **tissues**, **organs** and **systems**, as shown in the table.

Structure	Characteristics	Examples
Tissue	A large number of similar cells performing a particular function	• Plants: photosynthetic tissue, support tissue, root tissue etc. • Animals: skin tissue, muscle tissue, bone tissue, nerve tissue etc.
Organ	Two or more tissues grouped together, carrying out the same function.	• Stomach (epithelial, muscle and connective tissues) • Heart (muscle, blood and connective tissue).
System	Two or more organs working together with the same function.	• Digestive, circulatory, nervous, respiratory, excretory, reproductive and musculo-skeletal systems

• This **division of labour** between cells, tissues, organs and systems ensures that the multicellular organism functions smoothly and efficiently.

Common Errors

• Only animals have organs, plants do not.....they do. Examples of plant organs are the leaf, flower, root, stem etc.

Step II Be the Teacher

This question is followed by three model answers.

One of these answers is a Grade A answer (above 80% correct), another a Grade C answer (around 50% correct). The third answer could be any grade (A to E).

Mark all three answers giving an appropriate grade with reasoning.

Question

Distinguish, using the human circulatory system, the difference between system, organ and tissue.   [6 marks]

Answer 1

The circulatory system moves the blood around the body. The blood goes from one organ to another through the cells and tissues in the circulatory system.

Mark [ ]   Grade [ ]

Reasoning: ....
....
....

Answer 2

The circulatory system is a collection of organs like veins, arteries and heart. A system does a particular job like the circulatory system moves blood around the body. The heart pumps the blood as it has lots of muscle tissue. Organs have different tissues to do their job.

Muscle tissue is made up of lots muscle cells all doing the same job.

A cell is the unit that makes up a tissue.

Mark		Grade	

Reasoning: ....
....
....

Answer 3

System is a collection of organs.

Organ is a group of tissues doing a particular job. For example the heart.

Tissues are found throughout the body and help to link the organs together.

Mark		Grade	

Reasoning: ....
....

Actual Mark and Grade for Question

Answer 1

The circulatory system moves the blood around the body. The blood goes from one organ to another through the cells and tissues in the circulatory system.

Mark	1	Grade	E

Reasoning: Only one mark is scored for describing correctly what the circulatory system does (moves blood around the body). No second mark for describing system as a collection of organs.

No marks for saying an organ is a collection of tissues [1] and identifying an organ in the circulatory system (heart / blood vessels). [1]

No marks for saying a tissue is a number of similar cells doing a particular job [1] and giving an example, like muscle tissue in the heart. [1]

Answer 2

The circulatory system is a collection of organs like veins, arteries and heart. A system does a particular job like the circulatory system moves blood around the body. The heart pumps the blood as it has lots of muscle tissue. Organs have different tissues to do their job.

Muscle tissue is made up of lots muscle cells all doing the same job.

A cell is the unit that makes up a tissue.

Mark	6	Grade	A

Reasoning: All six possible marks are scored as follows:

Two marks for saying a system is a collection of organs [1] and explaining that the circulatory system pumps blood around the body. [1]

Two marks for saying an organ is a collection of tissues [1] and identifying an organ in the circulatory system (heart / blood vessels). [1]

Two marks for saying a tissue is a number of similar cells doing a particular job [1] and giving an example, like muscle tissue in the heart. [1]

Answer 3

System is a collection of organs

Organ is a collection of tissues doing a particular job. For example the heart.

Tissues are found throughout the body and help to link the organs together.

Mark	3		Grade	C

Reasoning: One mark for correctly describing a system (collection of organs). However no second mark for explaining what the circulatory system does.

Two marks for describing what an organ is (collection of tissues) and giving an example in the circulatory system (heart).

No marks for describing what a tissue is (similar cells doing a particular job) or giving an example in the circulatory system (muscle tissue, nerve tissue).

Step III Test Yourself

1. In each of these four terms one term is different from the other three and does not belong to the group. Identify the 'odd man out' giving your reasons.

    (a) nucleus   cell wall   vacuole   cytoplasm

    .... [2]

    (b) muscle   epithelial   nerve   stomach

    .... [2]

    (c) heart   excretory   respiratory   digestive |

    .... [2]

2. Cells have different shapes according to the particular job they do. Consider these four different shaped cells.

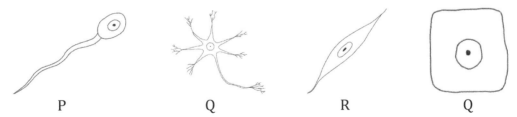

P   Q   R   Q

State which of these cells (P, Q, R or S) would be suitable for the following. Explain your choice.

Nerve cell .... [2]

Egg cell .... [2]

Sperm cell .... [2]

Muscle cell .... [2]

3. Match the bodily system to its correct description by drawing a line to link the two.

System	Description
Excretory •	• Breaking down of food
Circulatory •	• Carrying electrical impulses
Respiratory •	• Movement and support
Musculo-skeletal •	• Movement of blood around the body
Digestive •	• Removal of waste products
Nervous •	• Conversion of food into energy

[6]

MODEL ANSWERS

1. (a) Cell wall [1] as only found in plant cells. [1]

   (b) Stomach [1] is an organ [1], others are not.
   allow: others are all tissues.

   (c) Heart [1] is an organ [1], others are not.
   allow: others are all bodily systems.

2. Nerve cell is Q [1] because surrounding threads pick up electrical impulses. [1]
   allow: outer shape can pick up messages
   ignore: because of its shape

   Egg shell is S [1] because round shape allows it to travel easily to womb/uterus. [1]

   allow: can move easily
   ignore: because of its shape

   Sperm cell is P [1] because its tail allows it to travel from male through to egg in female. [1]
   allow: can move easily
   ignore: because of its shape

   Muscle cell is R [1] because its shape allows it to be stretched. [1]
   allow: can be pulled
   ignore: because of its shape

3.

Excretory	Breaking down of food	[1]
Circulatory	Carrying electrical impulses	[1]
Respiratory	Movement and support	[1]
Musculo-skeletal	Movement of blood around the body	[1]
Digestive	Removal of waste products	[1]
Nervous	Conversion of food into energy	[1]

The Particulate Nature of Matter

A. Particles of Matter
B. Particulate Model of Solids, Liquids and Gases
C. Particulate Model of Expansion, Contraction and Conservation of Mass

A. Particles of Matter

Step I Key Knowledge

- The material all around us is called **matter**. All matter is made up of **individual particles with spaces between the particles**. Matter is not continuous.

- Evidence that matter exists as particles comes from **diffusion**. This is the process of random movement of particles to fill a space. Diffusion occurs in liquids and gases.

Common Errors

- Solid particles are larger and heavier than liquid or gaseous particles.

  This is not necessarily true as solid elements are made up of atomic particles which are smaller than molecules of liquids or gases.

Step II Be the Teacher

This question is followed by three model answers.

One of these answers is a Grade A answer (above 80% correct), another a Grade C answer (around 50% correct). The third answer could be any grade (A to E).

Mark all three answers giving an appropriate grade with reasoning.

Questions

(a) Explain the meaning of diffusion. [2 marks]

(b) Explain why diffusion is evidence for matter existing as particles. [2 marks]

Answer 1

(a) Diffusion is the natural mixing of different gases or liquids.

(b) This can only happen if matter exists as particles with spaces between. The particles are constantly moving and this is how particles move from one place to another, through these spaces, which is diffusion

Mark [ ]   Grade [ ]

Reasoning:..
....
....
....
....

Answer 2

(a) Diffusion is the dissolving of a gas in a liquid.

(b) Spaces between the particles allows the dissolving to take place.

Mark [ ]   Grade [ ]

Reasoning:..
....
....
....
....

Answer 3

(a) Diffusion is the random movement of gases to fill the space available.

(b) Diffusion occurs best in gases and liquids.

Mark [ ]   Grade [ ]

Reasoning:..
....
....
....
....

Actual Mark and Grade for Question

Answer 1

(a) Diffusion is the natural mixing of different gases or liquids.

(b) This can only happen if matter exists as particles with spaces between. The particles are constantly moving and this is how particles move from one place to another, through these spaces, which is diffusion.

Mark	4		Grade	A

Reasoning: (a) Two marks for correct definition.

(b) Two marks for stating if particles then there must be space in between them [1]. The second mark is for saying particles are moving [1] randomly.

Answer 2

(a) Diffusion is the dissolving of a gas In a liquid.

(b) Spaces between the particles allows the dissolving to take place.

Mark	1		Grade	D

Reasoning: (a) No marks for definition.

(b) One mark for pointing out there is space between particles

---

Answer 3

(a) Diffusion is the random movement of gases to fill the space available.

(b) Diffusion occurs best in gases and liquids.

Mark	2		Grade	C

Reasoning: (a) Two marks for correct definition.

(b) No marks for evidence of particles.

Step III Test Yourself

1. (a) Perfume was placed on top of some liquid oil. It did not mix with the oil (immiscible) and floated on top. The oil was then very gently warmed. Explain in terms of particles why the smell of the perfume became stronger.

    ....

    ....

    .... [3]

    (b) (i) This time the perfume was added to *cold* water and it dissolved in the water. Would you expect the smell of the perfume to become stronger, less strong or not change. Explain you answer.

    ....

    ....

    .... [3]

    (ii) Complete the diagram to show how the particles of perfume and the particles of water are arranged in the aqueous solution of perfume.

perfume

aqueous solution
of perfume

water

[3]

    (c) Give a scientific explanation of why perfume is normally sprayed 'behind the ears' or on the 'wrist of a person'.

    ....

    ....

    .... [3]

1. (a) Heat energy from the oil causes the particles of perfume to move around more. [1] With greater energy some of these particles escape into the vapour phase. [1] In the vapour phase particles are moving around much more, so the smell of the perfume in the air is stronger. [1]

    (b) (i) Smell of perfume less strong. [1] This is because particles of perfume move less as they are colder. [1] Also the surrounding water molecules help prevent the perfume particles from escaping into the surrounding air. [1]

        (ii)

        Particles should be evenly spread out throughout the solution.   [3]

    (c) Both these areas are warm parts of the skin. [1] Body heat warms up the perfume [1] so it vaporises easily [1] to give off a pleasant aroma.

        allow: blood vessels warm the perfume, perfume changes to gas more easily

                                                                Total 12 marks

B. **Particulate Model of Solids, Liquids and Gases**

Step I Key Knowledge

• The **particulate theory of matter** states that all matter is made up of particles and that they are constantly **moving in a random manner**. As the particles are moving, they have **kinetic energy,** and the faster they move, the more energy they have.

• All **matter** is made up of individual particles such as molecules (compounds) or atoms (elements) which are arranged differently in **solids, liquids and gases**. The difference in behaviour of the particles in the three states is summarised in the table:

Property	Solid	Liquid	Gas
Arrangement of particles	Very closely packed together	Not so closely packed together	Very far apart with lots of space between the particles
Motion of particles	Vibrating in fixed positions	Moving about freely	Moving freely for relatively long distances
Volume and shape	Fixed volume and shape	Fixed volume but no fixed shape	No fixed volume and no fixed shape
Compressibility	Cannot be compressed	Cannot be compressed	Can be compressed

- A **change in state** is caused by a change in motion of the particles. A solid **melts** when its particles **gain energy** to move far apart like those in a liquid. In the same way, a liquid changes to a gas when its particles have gained even more energy to be even further apart. This is when a liquid **evaporates** or **boils** to become a gas.

- When a gas is **cooled,** its particles **lose energy,** coming closer together until they are close enough to show the properties of a liquid. This is **condensation**. Further cooling leads to the particles becoming very close and arranged in fixed positions as in a solid. This is **freezing** or solidification.

- The lowest temperature at which a substance changes from a solid to a liquid is called its **melting point**. The lowest temperature at which all of a liquid changes to a gas is called its **boiling point**.

- At **room temperature,** a substance is a **solid** if both its melting and boiling points are above room temperature. A substance is a **liquid** (at room temperature) if its melting point is below and its boiling point is above room temperature. A substance is a **gas** (at room temperature) if both its melting and boiling points are below room temperature.

Common Errors

- Solids have a certain shape as their particles are in a fixed shape and cannot move.

   This is untrue as their particles are vibrating about a fixed position which is movement. However unlike liquids or gases this movement is not random so solids retain their shape.

Step II Be the Teacher

This question is followed by three model answers

One of these answers is a Grade A answer (above 80% correct), another a Grade C answer (around 50% correct). The third answer could be any grade (A to E).

Mark all three answers giving an appropriate grade with reasoning.

Question

The graph shows the heating curve of a substance.

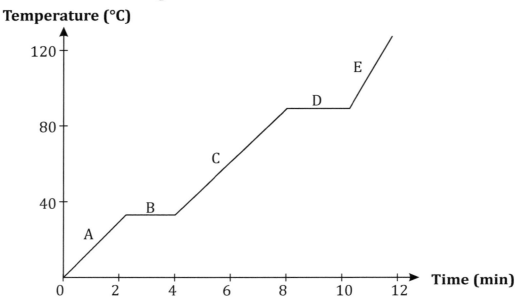

Identify the line segment (A, B, C, D or E) where you would you find the following:

(a) Both gas and liquid states. [1 mark]

(b) Solid state only [1 mark]

(c) Gaseous state only [1 mark]

(d) Both solid and liquid states. [1 mark]

(e) Particles closest together [1 mark]

(f) Particles furthest apart [1 mark]

Answer 1

(a) C and D   (b) A   (c) E   (d) C   (e) B   (f) E

Mark [　]   Grade [　]

Reasoning:...

....

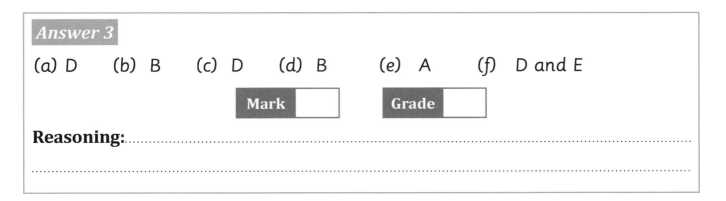

Answer 2

(a) D   (b) A   (c) E   (d) B   (e) A   (f) E

Mark	

Grade	

Reasoning: ....
....

Answer 3

(a) D   (b) B   (c) D   (d) B   (e) A   (f) D and E

Mark	

Grade	

Reasoning: ....
....

Actual Mark and Grade for Question 1

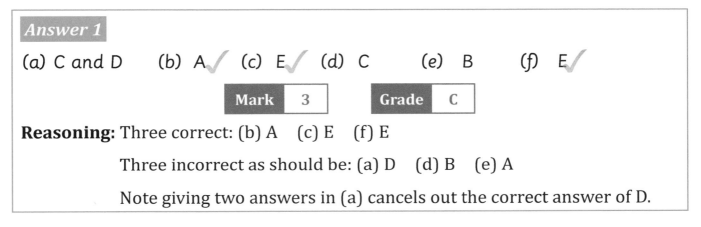

Answer 1

(a) C and D   (b) A ✓   (c) E ✓   (d) C   (e) B   (f) E ✓

Mark	3

Grade	C

Reasoning: Three correct: (b) A   (c) E   (f) E

Three incorrect as should be: (a) D   (d) B   (e) A

Note giving two answers in (a) cancels out the correct answer of D.

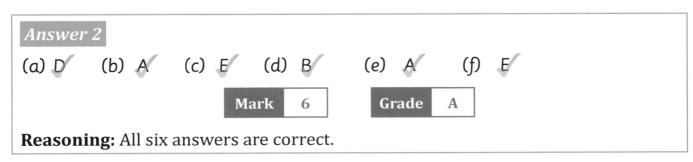

Answer 2

(a) D ✓   (b) A ✓   (c) E ✓   (d) B ✓   (e) A ✓   (f) E ✓

Mark	6

Grade	A

Reasoning: All six answers are correct.

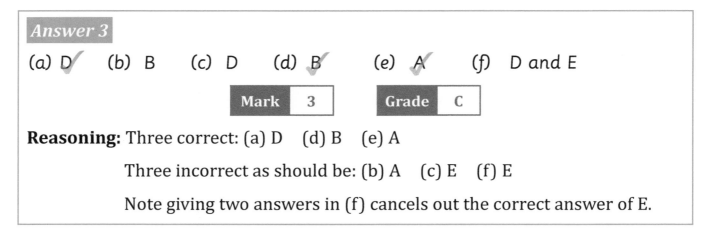

Answer 3

(a) D ✓   (b) B   (c) D   (d) B ✓   (e) A ✓   (f) D and E

Mark **3**   Grade **C**

Reasoning: Three correct: (a) D   (d) B   (e) A

Three incorrect as should be: (b) A   (c) E   (f) E

Note giving two answers in (f) cancels out the correct answer of E.

Step III Test Yourself

1. Below is a simple dichotomous key to identify the three states of matter.

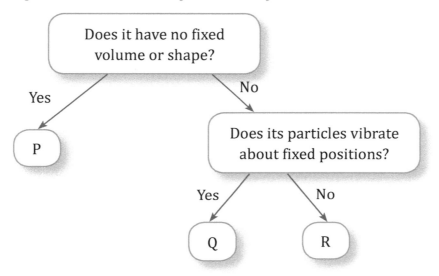

Identify the states P, Q and R.

P .... Q .... R .... [3]

2. Complete these revision notes about changes of state by adding these ten words in the appropriate place. Each word can only be used on one occasion.

vibrating	attractive	solid	liquid	melting point
freezing point	closer	further	gain	lose

On cooling a gas, the particles .... energy and become .... together. Eventually the gas becomes a .... Further cooling will change the liquid into a .... where the particles are just .... about fixed positions. The temperature at which all of a liquid changes to a solid is called its .... The temperature when all of a solid changes back to a liquid is called its .... This will require the particles to .... energy and become .... apart so the .... forces between the particles is less. [10]

3. Complete this table to compare the compressibility, motion of particles and volume and shape of the three states of matter.

	Compressibility	Motion of particles	Volume and shape
Solid	....	....	....
Liquid	....	....	....
Gas	....	....	....

[9]

MODEL ANSWERS

1. P...gas [1]   Q....solid [1]   R...liquid [1]

2. On cooling a gas, the particles **lose [1]** energy and become **closer [1]** together. Eventually the gas becomes a **liquid [1]**. Further cooling will change the liquid into a **solid [1]** where the particles are just **vibrating [1]** about fixed positions. The temperature at which all of a liquid changes to a solid is called its **freezing point [1]** The temperature when all of a solid changes back to a liquid is called its **melting point [1]** This will require the particles to **gain [1]** energy and become **further [1]** apart so the **attractive [1]** forces between the particles is less.

3.

	Compressibility	Motion of particles	Volume and shape
Solid	Cannot be compressed [1]	Vibrating about fixed positions [1]	Fixed volume and shape [1]
Liquid	Cannot be compressed [1]	Moving about freely [1]	Fixed volume but no fixed shape [1]
Gas	Can be compressed [1]	Moving freely for relatively long distances [1]	No fixed volume or shape [1]

Total 22 marks

C. Particulate Model of Expansion, Contraction and Conservation of Mass

Step I Key Knowledge

- **Expansion** takes place due to an **increase in temperature** which results in an **increase in the movement of the particles**.

> **Common Errors**
>
> - All materials expand by the same amount for a particular temperature rise.
>
>   This is untrue as different materials expand by different amounts. Expansion is always greatest in gases and least in solids.

- Different materials expand by different amounts. Expansion in **solids** is less than in liquids or gases. This is because in solids **the particles are vibrating about fixed positions.** During expansion the vibration is increased so the solid becomes slightly larger in size.

- In **gases** expansion is much greater as **the particles are free to move** and on heating move further apart increasing the volume and causing expansion.

- During **expansion** the **mass of the material is always conserved** as there is the same number of particles, just spaced further apart.

- **Contraction** is the opposite of expansion and is caused by a **decrease in temperature**. This results in less movement of the particles with a decrease in size.

- There is a **conservation of mass** during **contraction** as there is the same number of particles, just spaced closer together.

Step II Be the Teacher

This question is followed by three model answers.

One of these answers is a Grade A answer (above 80% correct), another a Grade C answer (around 50% correct). The third answer could be any grade (A to E).

Mark all three answers giving an appropriate grade with reasoning.

Question 1

Describe in terms of particles of matter what happens when a material is heated and expands. Explain the effect on the density of the material?   [4 marks]

Answer 1

When a material is heated its particles move around more. This causes the particles to become further apart. This then causes the density to increase as particles spread out more increasing the mass.

Mark [ ]   **Grade** [ ]

Reasoning: ....
....
....
....

Answer 2

When a material expands the particles move around more which makes the material hotter. More space between the particles increases volume which decreases density as the mass stays the same and density is mass/volume.

Mark [ ]   **Grade** [ ]

Reasoning: ....
....
....
....

Answer 3

Heating a material causes its particles to move around more so the same number of particles occupy a greater space. This has no effect on density as the total number of particles remains the same.

Mark [ ]   **Grade** [ ]

Reasoning: ....
....
....
....

Actual Mark and Grade for Question 1

Answer 1

When a material is heated its particles move around more. This causes the particles to become further apart. This then causes the density to increase as particles spread out more increasing the mass.

Mark	2		Grade	C

Reasoning: Scores 1 mark for particles moving more/faster and 1 mark for particles further apart.

No marks for density as this decreases because volume increases but mass remains constant.

Answer 2

When a material expands the particles move around more which makes the material hotter. More space between the particles increases volume which decreases density as the mass stays the same and density is mass/volume.

Mark	4		Grade	A

Reasoning: A good answer scoring all four marks for the following points:

- Particles moving more/faster
- Particles further apart/ more space between particles
- Volume increases
- Decrease in density

Answer 3

Heating a material causes its particles to move around more so the same number of particles occupy a greater space. This has no effect on density as the total number of particles remains the same.

Mark	2		Grade	C

Reasoning: Scores 1 mark for particles moving around more and 1 mark for occupying more space.

No marks were scored for explanation of density decrease due to increase in volume.

Question 2

3.2 g of copper powder was heated in a crucible. After three minutes it had completely changed into a black powder whose mass was 4.0 g. The table below shows how the mass changed with time.

Mass (g)	3.2	3.4	3.7	3.9	4.0	4.0	4.0
Time (min)	0.0	0.5	1.0	1.5	2.0	2.5	3.0

(a) Plot a graph to show how mass changed with time.   [6 marks]

(b) The copper powder has not expanded like a piece of copper metal but has undergone a chemical reaction.

Explain where the additional 0.8 g of mass has come from so the law of conservation of mass still applies.   [2 marks]

Answer 1

(a)

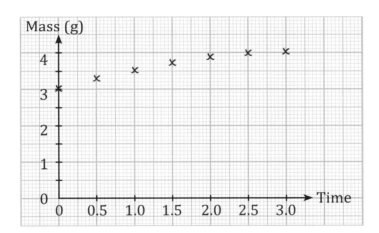

(b) The additional mass of 0.8 g has been added so the law of Conservation of Mass still applies. Always the mass of what you start with must equal the mass of what you end up with.

Mark [   ]   Grade [   ]

Reasoning:..

....

....

(a)

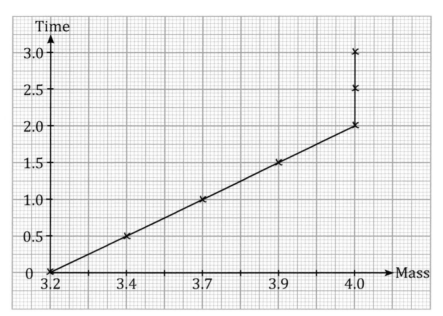

(b) A chemical reaction of heating the copper adds energy which adds the extra 0.8g of mass to the copper.

Mark		Grade	

Reasoning:...
....

(a)

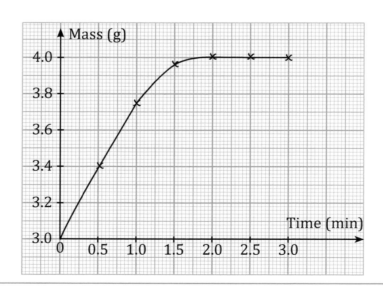

(b) The chemical reaction is with the oxygen in the air which combines with the copper to form black copper oxide. The extra mass is the oxygen.

Mark		Grade	

Reasoning:..
....
....

Actual Mark and Grade for Question 2

 Answer 1

(a)

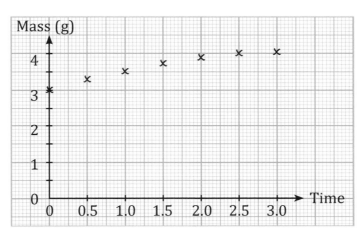

(b) The additional mass of 0.8 g has been added so the law of Conservation of Mass still applies. Always the mass of what you start with must equal the mass of what you end up with.

Mark	4	Grade	C

Reasoning: (a) 4 out of 6 marks for the graph. All the points are plotted correctly to score the 3 available marks. Time scale scores 1 mark. Mass scale loses one mark for not beginning at value 2 g or 3 g. 1 mark is also lost for not drawing the line of best fit.

(b) No marks are scored as the student has just recopied the question and stated the Law of Conservation of Mass. It is important to read the question which asks where the extra mass comes from. They have not explained that the extra mass is due to the gain in oxygen gas (1) from the air (1).

(a)

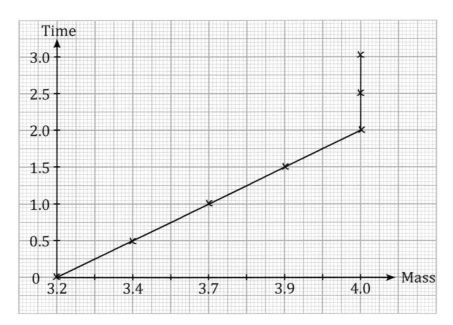

(b) A chemical reaction of heating the copper adds energy which adds the extra 0.8g of mass to the copper.

| Mark | 1 | | Grade | E |

Reasoning: (a) 1 out of 6 marks is scored for the graph. This one mark is for the time scale, even though it is on the wrong axis. Time should be plotted on the x axis as it is the independent variable in the experiment. Mass is the dependent variable and should be plotted on the y axis.

(b) No marks are scored as energy has no mass. You need to say that oxygen (1) is combined to the copper from the air (1).

Answer 3

(a)

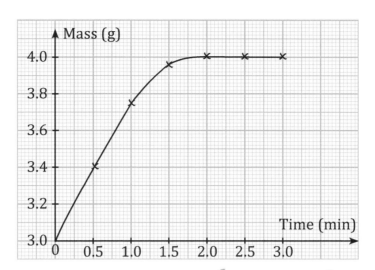

(b) The chemical reaction is with the oxygen in the air which combines with the copper to form black copper oxide. The extra mass is the oxygen.

| Mark | 8 | | Grade | A |

Reasoning: (a) All 6 marks are scored for the graph. 2 marks are for the correct mass/time scales. 3 marks for correctly plotting the seven points. 1 mark for correctly drawing the line of best fit. An excellent response

(b) Both marks are scored for correctly identifying that oxygen gas (1) from the air (1) has combined with the copper.

Step III Test Yourself

1. Explain in terms of particles why gases expand much more when they are heated than solids

....
....
....
.... [4]

2. Explain why if a solid expands it becomes larger but its mass does not increase.

....
....
....
.... [3]

3. The table shows the melting and boiling points of three substances.

	L	M	N
Melting point (°C)	−108	+144	−136
Boiling point (°C)	+64	+444	+1

(a) Identify which of these substances would expand the **most** for a certain temperature rise. Explain your choice.

.... [2]

(b) Identify which of these substances would expand the **least** for a certain temperature rise. Explain your choice.

.... [2]

MODEL ANSWERS

1. Gas particles can move freely [1] but solid particles are in fixed positions. [1] On heating gas particles move even further apart (large expansion). [1] However solid particles just vibrate more about fixed positions. This results in a small expansion [1]

   allow: heated particles gain energy, weak forces of attraction between gas particles, strong forces of attraction between solid particles

2. When a solid expands the number of particles remains the same. [1] No gain or loss of particles means the mass remains the same. [1] The particles just become slightly further apart which accounts for the expansion. [1]

   allow: expansion involves movement of particles,

3. (a) N expands most [1] as a gas. [1]
   ignore: both melting and boiling point below room temperature

   (b) M expands least [1] as solid. [1]
   ignore: both melting and boiling point above room temperature

   Total 11 marks

Atoms and Molecules

A. Atoms and Sub-Atomic Particles
B. Molecules and Compounds
C. Chemical Formula

A. Atoms and Sub-Atomic Particles

Step I Key Knowledge

- An **atom** is the **smallest particle of an element**. Atoms of an element are all identical. For example, one atom of hydrogen would be identical to all other atoms of hydrogen. However, it would be different from an atom of oxygen or an atom of iron.

- As there are more than 100 different atoms (more than 100 elements), scientists use **chemical symbols** to represent atoms. The chemical symbol is usually the first or first and second letters of its name (sometimes Latin name).

- An atom is a neutral particle and it is made up of three **sub-atomic particles: proton, neutron** and **electron**.

- **Protons** and **neutrons** are tightly packed together in the **nucleus**. They are not free to move. Electrons are much smaller and orbit around the nucleus. A summary of the properties of the sub-atomic particles is shown in the table.

Sub-atomic particle	Symbol	Relative mass	Relative charge
Proton	p	1	+1
Neutron	n	1	0
Electron	e	1/2000	-1

Common Errors

- Atoms always have equal numbers of protons and neutrons.

  Some atoms do but not all. Atoms are electrically neutral so always have the same number of protons (+) and electrons (-). The number of neutrons can be the same or higher than the number of protons.

- Atoms of the **same element** always contain the **same number of protons** and those of different elements contain different numbers of protons.

- An element is identified by its **proton number** (which is also called its **atomic number**). On the Periodic Table of Elements, it is the lower (smaller) number next to the chemical symbol.

$$\text{Mass number} \longrightarrow \overset{23}{\underset{11}{\text{Na}}} \longleftarrow$$

Mass number $\longrightarrow$ 23

Na

Proton number $\longrightarrow$ 11

- All atoms have the same number of electrons as protons. Hence, the proton number also indicates the number of electrons in the atom.

- The **mass number** of the atom is the **total number of protons and neutrons in the nucleus**. Therefore, the difference between the mass number and the proton number of an element is the number of neutrons in the nucleus of that element.

Step II Be the Teacher

This question is followed by three model answers.

One of these answers is a Grade A answer (above 80% correct), another a Grade C answer (around 50% correct). The third answer could be any grade (A to E).

Mark all three answers giving an appropriate grade with reasoning.

Questions

(a) Draw a table to compare the relative charge and relative mass of the three sub-atomic particles, protons, neutrons and electrons found in atoms.   [6 marks]

(b) Identify and name the elements below that have an equal number of protons, neutrons and electrons.

$$^{11}_{5}\text{B} \qquad ^{14}_{7}\text{N} \qquad ^{32}_{16}\text{S} \qquad ^{39}_{19}\text{K} \qquad ^{80}_{35}\text{Br}$$

[2 marks]

Answer 1

(a)

	Proton	Neutron	Electron
Relative mass	0	0	1
Relative charge	1	0	1

(b) $^{14}_{7}\text{N}$ $^{32}_{16}\text{S}$

Mark		Grade	

Reasoning: ....
....
....

Answer 2

(a)

	Relative charge	Relative mass
Proton	1	+1
Neutron	0	−1
Electron	1	0

(b) $^{14}_{7}\text{N}$ nitrogen $^{32}_{16}\text{S}$ sulfur

| Mark | | Grade | |

Reasoning:..

....

....

....

....

Answer 3

(a)

Proton	Relative mass = 1	Relative charge = +1
Neutron	Relative mass = 1	Relative charge = 0
Electron	Relative mass = 1/2000	Relative charge = −1

(b) nitrogen and sulphur

| Mark | | Grade | |

Reasoning:..

....

....

....

Actual Mark and Grade for Question

Answer 1

(a)

	Proton	*Neutron*	*Electron*
Relative mass	0	0	1
Relative charge	1	0 ✓	1

(b) $^{14}_{7}N$ $^{32}_{16}S$

| Mark | 1 | | Grade | E |

Reasoning: (a) In the table only the relative charge of the neutron scores 1 mark. The relative charge of the proton must be +1 and electron -1, not just 1.

(b) No marks are scored as the questions asks you to 'name the element' that contains equal numbers of protons, neutrons and electrons. It is very important to read the question carefully and do as requested.

Answer 2

(a)

	Relative charge	*Relative mass*
Proton	1	+1
Neutron	0 ✓	−1
Electron	1	0 ✓

(b) $^{14}_{7}N$ nitrogen ✓  $^{32}_{16}S$ sulfur ✓

| Mark | 4 | | Grade | C |

Reasoning: (a) Table scores 2 marks for correct relative charge of neutron and relative mass of electron. The other answers have incorrect + or – signs with the mass and omit + and – signs with the charge.

(b) Both marks are scored as they are correctly named. Nitrogen contains 7 protons / 7 neutrons / 7 electrons and sulfur contains 16 protons / 16 neutrons / 16 electrons.

Answer 3

(a)

Proton	Relative mass = 1 ✓	Relative charge = +1 ✓
Neutron	Relative mass = 1 ✓	Relative charge = 0 ✓
Electron	Relative mass = 1/2000 ✓	Relative charge = –1 ✓

(b) nitrogen ✓ (7 of each sub-atomic particle) and sulphur ✓ (16 of each sub-atomic particle)

Mark	8		Grade	A

Reasoning: Commendable answer with all 8 marks scored in question. It is acceptable for electron to have 0 mass or more accurately 1/2000.

Step III Test Yourself

1. Below is a dichotomous key to identify sub-atomic particles.

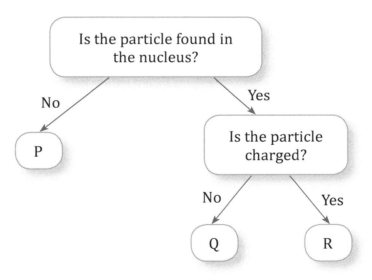

Identify the three sub-atomic particles P, Q and R.

P ....   Q ....   R ....   [3]

2. Complete the table below.

Atom	Number of protons	Number of neutrons	Number of electrons
$^{1}_{1}H$			
$^{23}_{11}Na$			
$^{39}_{19}K$			

[9]

3. Eight students were discussing sub-atomic particles. Below are the statements the students made.

Yulin: The proton number is also called the atomic number.

Hui Li: A neutron is a positively charged particle found in the nucleus.

Rowarti: An electron is a positively charged particle.

Uma: The total number of protons and electrons is the mass number.

Weimin: Protons orbit around the nucleus.

Wenyong: The number of protons is equal to the number of neutrons.

Tingting: Neutron particles have negligible mass.

Fenfang: The nucleus comprises of neutrons and electrons.

(a) Only one student made a completely correct statement. Who is the student?

.... [1]

(b) The other seven statements can easily be corrected by changing just **one word**. Write down the corrected statements.

....

....

....

....

....

....

.... [7]

MODEL ANSWERS

1. P = electron [1]   Q = neutron [1]   R = proton [1]

2.

Atom	Number of protons		Number of neutrons		Number of electrons	
$^{1}_{1}\text{H}$	1	[1]	0	[1]	1	[1]
$^{23}_{11}\text{Na}$	11	[1]	12	[1]	11	[1]
$^{39}_{19}\text{K}$	19	[1]	20	[1]	19	[1]

3. (a) **Yulin** [1]

   (b) **Hui Li:**   A neutron is a **neutral** [1] charged particle found in the nucleus.

   Rowarti: An electron is a **negatively** [1] charged particle.

   Uma: The total number of protons and **neutrons** [1] is the mass number.

   Weimin: **Electrons** [1] orbit around the nucleus.

   Wenyong: The number of protons is equal to the number of **electrons** [1].

   Tingting: **Electron** [1] particles have negligible mass.

   Fenfang: The nucleus comprises of neutrons and **protons** [1].

   Total 20 marks

B. Molecules and Compounds

Step I Key Knowledge

- **Molecules** are formed when **atoms combine together**. These molecules may contain atoms of the same element or atoms of different elements.

- A molecule of an **element** consists of a **fixed number** of only **one kind of atom** chemically combined together. For example hydrogen gas (H_2) or oxygen gas (O_2).

- A **compound** consists of a **fixed number** of **different kinds of atoms** chemically combined together. For example, a molecule of water consists of two hydrogen atoms chemically joined to an oxygen atom (H_2O)

Common Errors

- Molecules are always compounds….. they are not.

    A molecule is atoms chemically joined together. The atoms may be the same and the result is a molecule of an element eg O_2 (oxygen gas). If the atoms joined together come from different elements then the molecule is a compound eg H_2O (water).

Step II Be the Teacher

This question is followed by three model answers.

One of these answers is a Grade A answer (above 80% correct), another a Grade C answer (around 50% correct). The third answer could be any grade (A to E).

Mark all three answers giving an appropriate grade with reasoning.

Question

Distinguish between a molecule of an element and a molecule of a compound, using the molecules given below. Name each of the molecules shown.

CO_2 I_2 H_2O Br_2 [6 Marks]

Answer 1

Molecules of elements always have two atoms but molecules of compounds have more than two atoms.

????????   iodine   water   bromine

Mark		Grade	

Reasoning: ....

....

....

Answer 2

Molecules of elements only contain one type of atom but molecules of compounds contain atoms of different elements.

Iodine and bromine are elements but carbon oxide and hydrogen oxide are compounds.

Mark		Grade	

Reasoning:..

....

....

Answer 3

A molecule of a compound contains different atoms of different elements. A molecule of an element contains only the same type of atom. For example iodine (I_2) and bromine (Br_2) are elements as same atoms, but carbon dioxide (CO_2) and water (H_2O) are compounds as different atoms.

Mark		Grade	

Reasoning:..

....

....

Actual Mark and Grade for Question

Answer 1

Molecules of elements always have two atoms but molecules of compounds have more than two atoms.

????????   iodine ✓   water ✓   bromine ✓

Mark	3	Grade	C

Reasoning: Scores 3 marks for correctly identifying iodine, water and bromine.

Although iodine and bromine each contain two atoms it is not the reason they are elements. The reason they are elements is they contain the same type of atoms. For example HCl contains two atoms but it is not an element but a compound called hydrogen chloride.

Answer 2

Molecules of elements only contain one type of atom but molecules of compounds contain atoms of different elements.

Iodine and bromine are elements but carbon oxide and hydrogen oxide are compounds

<table>
<tr><td>Mark</td><td>4</td><td>Grade</td><td>B</td></tr>
</table>

Reasoning: Scores both marks for correctly distinguishing molecules of elements and molecules of compounds.

Scores another two marks for correctly naming iodine and bromine molecules. Need to say carbon dioxide and water to score other two marks.

Answer 3

A molecule of a compound contains different atoms of different elements. A molecule of an element contains only the same type of atom. For example iodine (I_2) and bromine (Br_2) are elements as same atoms, but carbon dioxide (CO_2) and water (H_2O) are compounds as different atoms.

<table>
<tr><td>Mark</td><td>6</td><td>Grade</td><td>A</td></tr>
</table>

Reasoning: A model answer scoring all 6 marks.

Step III Test Yourself

1. Choose only from the following molecules.

$$O_3 \qquad N_2O_4 \qquad N_2 \qquad C_2H_4 \qquad HNO_3 \qquad SO_2$$

(a) State which of these are molecules of elements.

.... [2]

(b) State which of these molecules contain two elements.

.... [3]

(c) State which of these molecules contains 3 atoms.

.... [2]

(d) State which of these molecules contains 6 atoms.

.... [2]

(e) Identify which of these molecules is called

    (i) nitrogen gas .... [1]

    (ii) sulfur dioxide .... [1]

2. ◇ □ ○ represent atoms of different elements. Molecules containing these atoms are shown below.

    L   M   N   O   P

(a) Identify which of these are molecules of compounds............................ [3]

(b) Identify which of these could be a molecule of water. .... [1]

(c) Identify which of these could be a molecule of oxygen gas. .... [1]

3. Compounds are formed when atoms combine together. Complete the following chemical equations by filling in the spaces.

(a) .... + ... → sulfur dioxide [2]

(b) .... + ... → calcium chloride [2]

MODEL ANSWERS

1. (a) O_3 [1], N_2 [1]

    (b) N_2O_4 [1], C_2H_4 [1], SO_2 [1]

    (c) O_3 [1], SO_2 [1]

    (d) N_2O_4 [1], C_2H_4 [1]

    (e) (i) N_2 [1], (ii) SO_2 [1]

2. (a) L [1], M [1] and O [1], (b) O [1], (c) P [1]

3. (a) sulfur [1] + oxygen [1] → sulfur dioxide

    ignore: oxide for oxygen

    (b) calcium [1] + chlorine [1] → calcium chloride

    ignore: chloride for chlorine

Total 20 marks

C. Chemical Formula

Step I Key Knowledge

- A symbol called a **chemical formula** is used to represent a **molecule of an element or compound**. For example, H_2O represents a molecule of water. This shows the component elements as well as the ratio of different atoms that make up the compound.

- **Chemical formulas** are also used to represent the composition of other compounds that are not molecules. For example magnesium sulfate has a chemical formula of $MgSO_4$. This indicates that the ratio of atoms in the compound are 1 sulfur, 1 magnesium and 4 oxygen.

- **Chemical formulas** are used in **chemical equations** to represent **chemical change**. For example hydrogen gas burning in oxygen gas to form water.

$$2H_2 + O_2 \rightarrow 2H_2O$$

Common Errors

- Compounds have different chemical formulas depending on how they were made. This is incorrect as the chemical formula of a compound is always the same, however it is made. Compounds have a fixed chemical composition.

Step II Be the Teacher

This question is followed by three model answers.

One of these answers is a Grade A answer (above 80% correct), another a Grade C answer (around 50% correct). The third answer could be any grade (A to E).

Mark all three answers giving an appropriate grade with reasoning.

Questions

Consider only these six chemical formulae.

H_2SO_4 CH_4 N_2 $C_6H_{12}O_6$ CO_2 NH_3

Each formula can only be used once as an answer to the following questions.

(a) State the name of the formula which contains 4 atoms in its molecule.   [1 mark]

(b) State the name of the formula of the molecule that is the most abundant gas in the air.   [1 mark]

(c) State the name of the formula of the molecule that is the main cause of global warming.   [1 mark]

(d) Write down the formula of the molecule which has a sweet taste.   [1 mark]

(e) Write down the formula of the molecule which is an acid.   [1 mark]

(f) Write down the formula of the molecule which is highly flammable. [1 mark]

Answer 1

(a) NH_3 (b) N_2 (c) CO_2

(d) $C_6H_{12}O_6$ (e) H_2SO_4 (f) CH_4

Mark [   ]   Grade [   ]

Reasoning: ....
....
....

Answer 2

(a) ammonia (NH_3)   (b) nitrogen (N_2)   (c) Carbon dioxide (CO_2)

(d) H_2SO_4 (e) CH_4 (f) $C_6H_{12}O_6$

Mark [   ]   Grade [   ]

Reasoning: ....
....
....

Answer 3

(a) ammonia (NH_3)   (b) nitrogen (N_2)   (c) Carbon dioxide (CO_2)

(d) $C_6H_{12}O_6$ (e) H_2SO_4 (f) CH_4

Mark [   ]   Grade [   ]

Reasoning: ....
....
....

Actual Mark and Grade for Question

Answer 1

(a) NH_3 (b) N_2 (c) CO_2

(d) $C_6H_{12}O_6$ ✓ (e) H_2SO_4 ✓ (f) CH_4 ✓

Mark	3		Grade	C

Reasoning: (a), (b) and (c) do not score as question asked for name of the molecule, not its formula. It is important to read the question thoroughly and follow all instructions carefully.

(d), (e) and (f) score three marks for correct formula of sweet glucose ($C_6H_{12}O_6$), sulfuric acid (H_2SO_4) and flammable methane (CH_4).

Answer 2

(a) ammonia (NH_3) ✓ (b) nitrogen (N_2) ✓ (c) Carbon dioxide (CO_2) ✓

(d) H_2SO_4 (e) CH_4 (f) $C_6H_{12}O_6$

Mark	3		Grade	C

Reasoning: (a), (b) and (c) score three marks but the last three are incorrect. (d) $C_6H_{12}O_6$ is sweet glucose sugar (e) H_2SO_4 is sulfuric acid (f) CH_4 is flammable methane gas (main component of natural gas)

Answer 3

(a) ammonia (NH_3) ✓ (b) nitrogen (N_2) ✓ (c) Carbon dioxide (CO_2) ✓

(d) $C_6H_{12}O_6$ ✓ (e) H_2SO_4 ✓ (f) CH_4 ✓

Mark	6		Grade	A

Reasoning: Commendable answer with all six marks scored.

Step III Test Yourself

1. A chemical formula represents the number of atoms present in a molecule of the chemical compound. Write the chemical formula of the following chemical compounds.

(a) Molecule with two hydrogens and one sulfur atom. .... [1]

(b) Molecule with two nitrogens and four oxygen atoms. .... [1]

(c) Molecule with two hydrogens, one sulfur and four oxygen atoms. .... [1]

2. Complete the table about the chemical formula of certain compounds.

Name of chemical compound	Name of metal present	Name of non-metal(s) present	Chemical formula
Carbon dioxide	none	....	....
Calcium carbonate	....	....	$CaCO_3$
Copper sulfate	....	....	$CuSO_4$
....	....	....	NaCl
....	....	....	$MgCO_3$

[12]

MODEL ANSWERS

1. (a) H_2S [1] (b) N_2O_4 [1] (c) H_2SO_4 [1]

2.

Name of chemical compound	Name of metal present	Name of non-metal(s) present	Chemical formula
Carbon dioxide	none	carbon, oxygen [1]	CO_2 [1]
Calcium carbonate	calcium [1]	carbon, oxygen [1]	$CaCO_3$
Copper sulfate	copper [1]	sulfur, oxygen [1]	$CuSO_4$
Sodium chloride [1]	sodium [1]	chlorine [1]	NaCl
Magnesium carbonate [1]	magnesium [1]	carbon, oxygen [1]	$MgCO_3$

Ray Model of Light

A. Light and Shadow
B. Reflection of Light
C. Refraction of Light
D. Dispersion of Light and Colour

A. Light and Shadow

Step I Key Knowledge

- **Light** is a **form of energy** that enables us to see. It can travel through a vacuum (empty space) and has a **speed** of about **300 million metres per second**.

- Objects that give out light energy are said to be **luminous objects**. Examples are the Sun, stars, an electric lamp and a candle.

- **Light travels in straight lines** along paths which are called **light rays**. A bundle of light rays is called a **beam** of light.

- A **shadow** is an area of darkness on the surface. It is formed when an **opaque** object (one that does not allow light to pass through) prevents light from falling on that surface.

- An **eclipse** is the total or partial blocking of sunlight when one celestial body (Earth or Moon) passes in between the Sun and the other celestial body.

Common Errors

- Moonlight is light given off by the Moon.

  This is incorrect as the Moon produces no light. What we see as moonlight is sunlight that has been reflected off the Moon on to the Earth.

Step II Be the Teacher

This question is followed by three model answers.

One of these answers is a Grade A answer (above 80% correct), another a Grade C answer (around 50% correct). The third answer could be any grade (A to E).

Mark all three answers giving an appropriate grade with reasoning.

Question

Draw light rays on the diagram below to show how shadow forms on the Earth in a solar eclipse. In the diagram you draw distinguish between a partial and total eclipse on Earth.

Answer 1

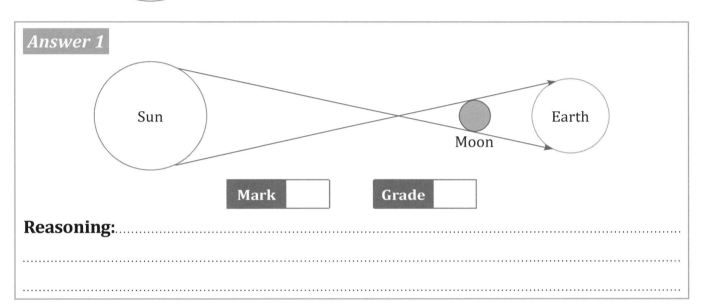

Mark		Grade	

Reasoning:..
....
....

Answer 2

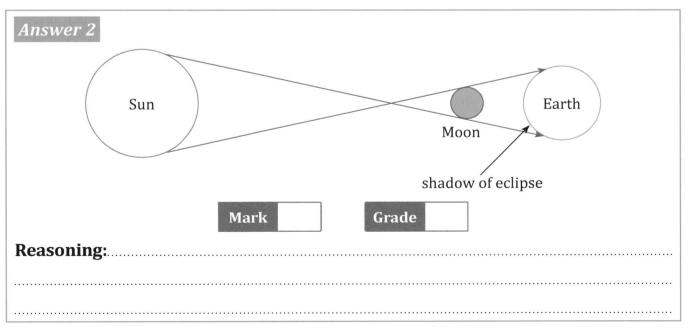

shadow of eclipse

Mark		Grade	

Reasoning:..
....
....

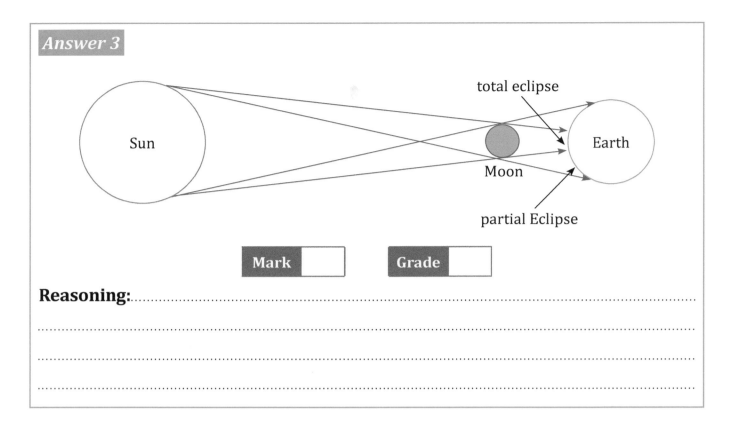

Answer 3

Sun — total eclipse — Moon — Earth — partial Eclipse

Mark [ ] Grade [ ]

Reasoning: ....
....
....
....

Actual Mark and Grade for Question

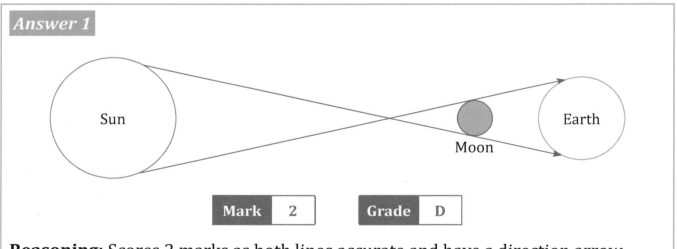

Answer 1

Sun — Moon — Earth

Mark [2] Grade [D]

Reasoning: Scores 2 marks as both lines accurate and have a direction arrow.

However no distinction between partial and total eclipse and no labelling of eclipse/shadow.

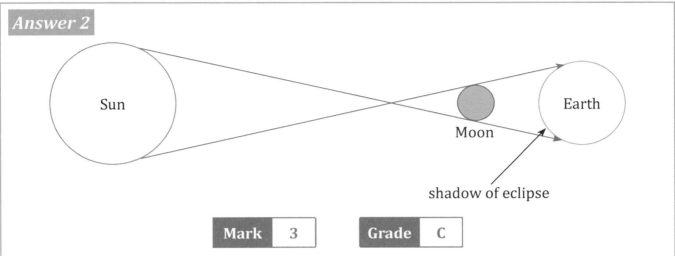

Mark 3   **Grade** C

Reasoning: 3 marks scored as correctly shows shadow of eclipse. This is a partial eclipse.

No light rays drawn to show the formation of a total eclipse.

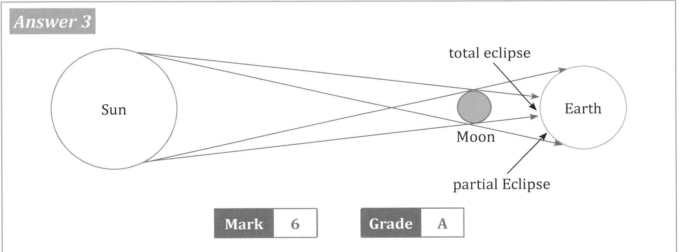

Mark 6   **Grade** A

Reasoning: Scores full marks as correctly covers both partial and total eclipse. Both are clearly labelled and drawn. An excellent response.

Step III Test Yourself

1. An experiment was set up to investigate the size of a shadow from an opaque object. The arrangement used is shown below. You may assume that the small light bulb acts as a point source of light.

    (a) Mark on the screen where the shadow of the opaque object occurs. [2]

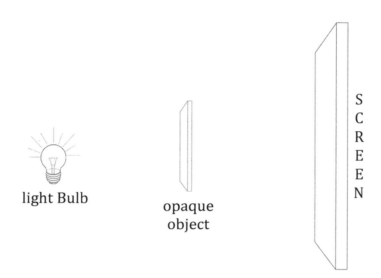

light Bulb

opaque object

S
C
R
E
E
N

(b) The table shows some results from the experiment using a 2 cm opaque object. It shows the size of the shadow formed when the object and screen are different distances from the light bulb.

(i) Complete the table of the missing values.

Opaque object size	Size of shadow on screen	Distance of object from light bulb	Distance of screen from light bulb
2 cm	4 cm	4 cm	8 cm
2 cm	8 cm	4 cm	....
2 cm	....	10 cm	40 cm
2 cm	10 cm	....	50 cm

[3]

(ii) What is the relationship between the size of the shadow and the position of the screen?

....

.... [2]

(c) The size of the opaque object was then changed and further results recorded. Complete the table of missing values.

Opaque object size	Size of shadow on screen	Distance of object from light bulb	Distance of screen from light bulb
3 cm	12 cm	4 cm	16 cm
5 cm	20 cm	....	40 cm
8 cm	....	50 cm	150 cm
....	8 cm	20 cm	40 cm

[3]

MODEL ANSWERS

1. (a)

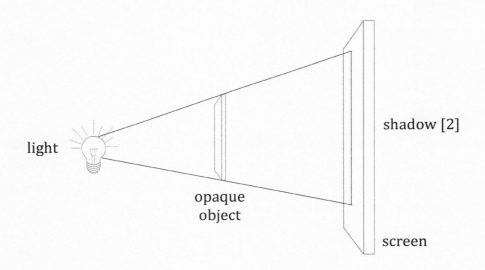

light

opaque object

shadow [2]

screen

(b) (i)

Opaque object size	Size of shadow on screen	Distance of object from light bulb	Distance of screen from light bulb
2 cm	4 cm	4 cm	8 cm
2 cm	8 cm	4 cm	16 cm [1]
2 cm	8 cm [1]	10 cm	40 cm
2 cm	10 cm	10 cm [1]	50 cm

(ii) If you double [1] the distance of the screen from the opaque object the size of the shadow also doubles. [1]

allow: size of shadow is directly proportional to the distance of screen from object [2], as screen moves away shadow gets bigger [1]

ignore: shadow gets bigger on its own, distance gets larger on its own

(c)

Opaque object size	Size of shadow on screen	Distance of object from light bulb	Distance of screen from light bulb
3 cm	12 cm	4 cm	16 cm
5 cm	20 cm	10 cm [1]	40 cm
8 cm	24 cm [1]	50 cm	150 cm
4 cm [1]	8 cm	20 cm	40 cm

Total 10 marks

B. Reflection of Light

Step I Key Knowledge

- **Reflection is the bouncing off of light from an object**. Light is reflected from a mirror in the same way as a ball is bounced off a smooth floor. A light ray is reflected off a mirror at the same angle it hits the mirror. **The incident angle is always the same as the reflected angle**.

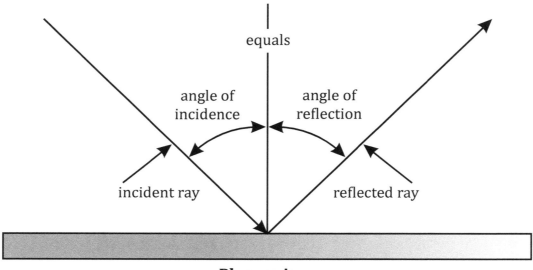

Plane mirror

Common Errors

- The angle of incidence is the angle that the ray of light makes to the surface of the mirror. This is incorrect.

  The angle of incidence is the angle the ray of light makes to the normal ray which is at 90° to the surface of the mirror.

- When you look in a **plane mirror** you will see your image in the mirror. When you raise your left hand, the right hand in the mirror will be raised. Mirrors turn images around from left to right. We say the image of plane mirrors is **laterally inverted**.

- If you try to capture the image which appears behind the mirror by putting it on a screen, you will be unsuccessful. We call this type of image that cannot be captured on a screen a **virtual image**. All plane mirrors produce virtual images.

- In summary, the images of plane mirrors are:

  - ➤ **Upright**.

  - ➤ **Laterally inverted** (turned from left to right).

  - ➤ **Virtual** (cannot be captured on a screen).

  - ➤ Always the **same size** as the object.

  - ➤ Always the **same distance behind the mirror** as the object is in front.

Step II Be the Teacher

This question is followed by three model answers.

One of these answers is a Grade A answer (above 80% correct), another a Grade C answer (around 50% correct). The third answer could be any grade (A to E).

Mark all three answers giving an appropriate grade with reasoning.

Questions

(a) Complete the ray diagram to show the position of the image formed in the plane mirror of the man. **[5 Marks]**

(b) Explain what is meant by this image being virtual. **[1 mark]**

(a)

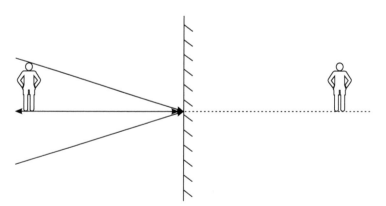

(b) Virtual means it is not real

Mark		Grade	

Reasoning: ....

....

....

....

....

Answer 2

(a)

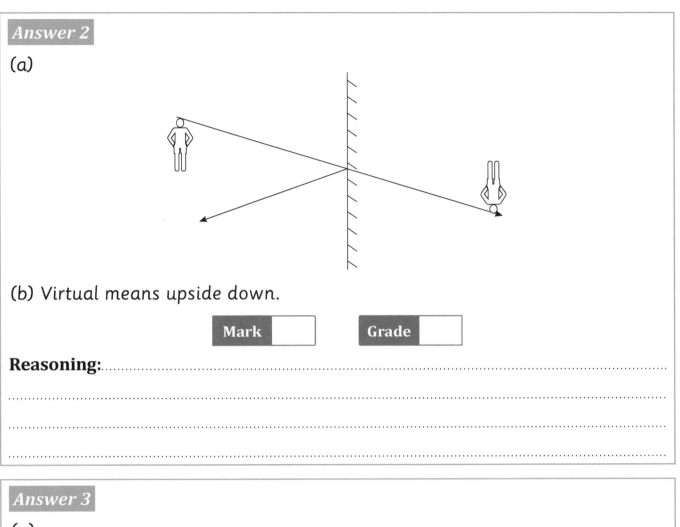

(b) Virtual means upside down.

Mark		Grade	

Reasoning: ....
....
....
....

Answer 3

(a)

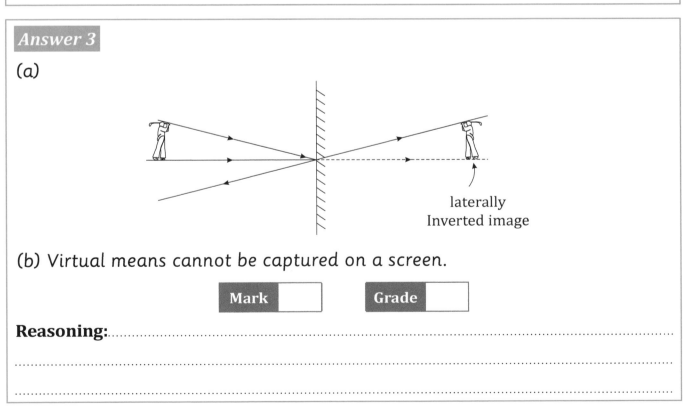

laterally
Inverted image

(b) Virtual means cannot be captured on a screen.

Mark		Grade	

Reasoning: ....
....
....

Actual Mark and Grade for Question

Answer 1

(a)

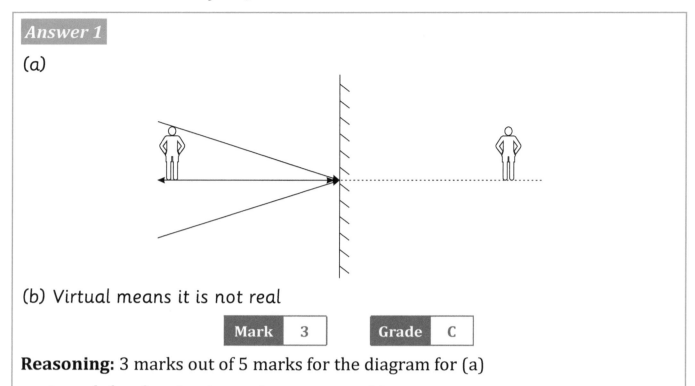

(b) Virtual means it is not real

Mark	3		Grade	C

Reasoning: 3 marks out of 5 marks for the diagram for (a)

- 1 mark for showing image in correct position
- 1 mark for showing image laterally inverted
- 1 mark for showing correct reflected ray

No mark for (b) as need to say 'image cannot be captured on screen'.

Answer 2

(a)

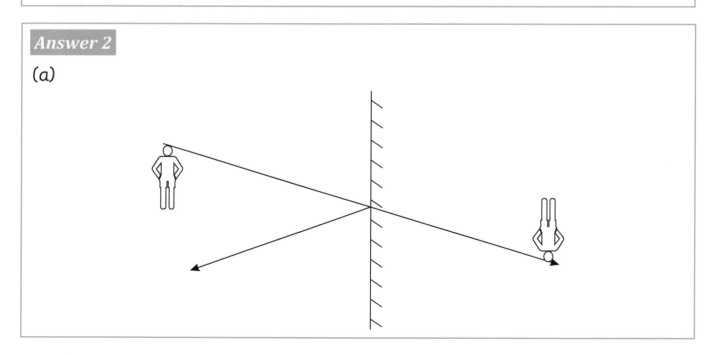

(b) Virtual means upside down.

Mark	1	Grade	E

Reasoning: (a) Only one mark scored for showing correct reflected ray.

(b) No mark scored as image is not upside down but is laterally inverted.

Answer 3

(a)

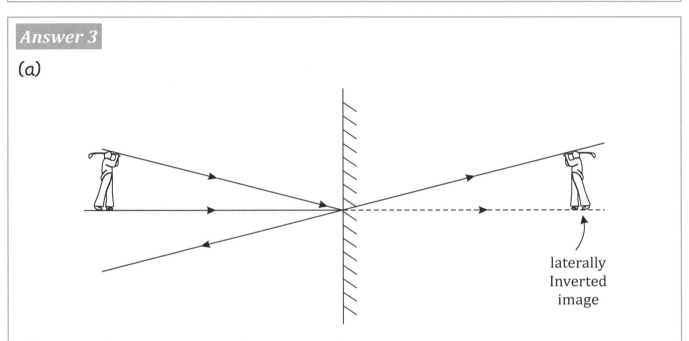

laterally
Inverted
image

(b) Virtual means cannot be captured on a screen.

Mark	6	Grade	A

Reasoning: (a) Excellent drawing with all five marks being scored for these points:

- Correct incident ray
- Correct reflected ray carried through
- Correct normal ray carried through.
- Correct position of image
- Showing image is laterally inverted

(b) 1 mark for correct answer that virtual means 'cannot be captured on screen'.

Step III Test Yourself

1. Images in a plane mirror are laterally inverted. In the boxes below show what the six letters of the word POLICE would look like if viewed in a mirror.

[4]

2. The periscope of a submarine has two plane mirrors to help the sailors see above the water.

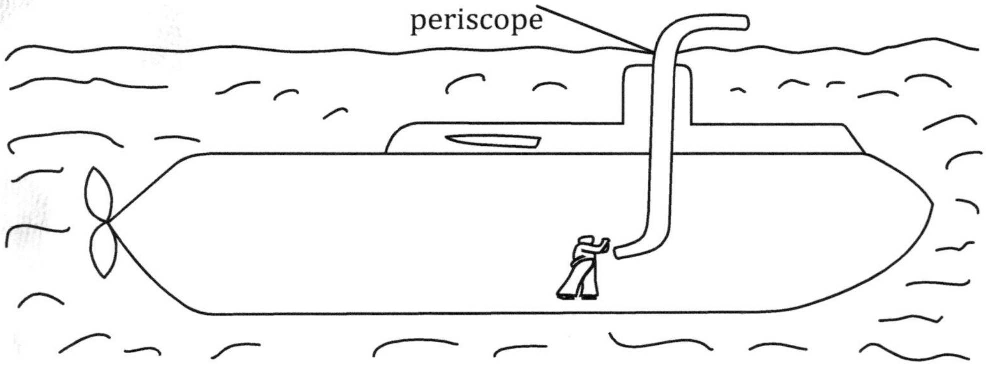

(a) Draw a diagram of the two plane mirrors to show how the light is reflected.

[3]

(b) (i) State the angle of incidence of the light at each of the mirrors.

   .... [1]

   (ii) State the angle of reflection of the light at each of the mirrors.

   .... [1]

(iii) Identify the angle the light is turned through by each plane mirror.

.... [1]

(c) Give two other uses of periscopes.

1. ....

2. .... [2]

3. The diagram shows a cross-section of a 20 cm x 10 cm pinhole camera. An object 100 cm tall is held 2 m in front of the pinhole camera.

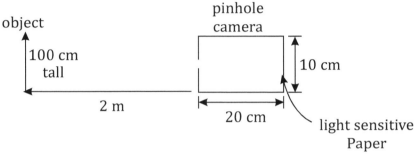

(a) State whether the image formed on the light sensitive paper is upright or inverted.

.... [1]

(b) The image that forms on the light sensitive paper is exactly 10 cm tall. Explain this using the object and image distances given and the original height of the object.

....

.... [2]

MODEL ANSWERS

1. Deduct one mark for each incorrect letter. [4]

q	O	ꓶ	I	Ɔ	Ǝ

2. (a)

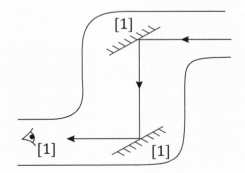

(b) (i) 45° [1]   (ii) 45° [1]   (iii) 90° [1]

(c) looking over walls [1] looking around corners [1]

allow: looking over or around or under any object

ignore: looking up, looking around, looking under

3. (a) inverted   [1]

   (b) The object distance is 200 cm which is 10x greater than the image distance of 20 cm.   [1]

   Therefore the object size (100 cm) will be 10x bigger than the image size (10 cm).   [1]

   allow: ratio of distance (object/image) to size (object/image) is same

                                                                        Total 15 marks

C. Refraction of Light

Step I Key Knowledge

- **Refraction is the bending of light** as it passes from one transparent material to another of different density.

> **Common Errors**
>
> - Light rays that hit a transparent medium at 90° are bounced back.
>
> This is not so as these light rays pass straight through the transparent medium without deviation.

- **Refraction** is caused by a **change in the speed of light** as it passes through a different transparent medium. When light travels from the air through a glass block, it slows down and is bent towards the normal (see diagram). When the light leaves the glass block, its speed increases and it bends away from the normal.

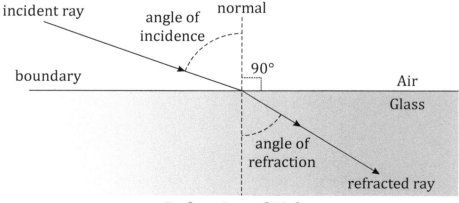

Refraction of Light

Common Errors

- Light like sound travels faster through transparent solids. This is false.

Light travels slower through transparent solids so is bent inwards towards the normal line at the surface. This results in the refraction (bending) of the light.

- The **effects of refraction** are:
  - ➤ **Objects in water** or underneath glass **appear closer to the surface** than they actually are.
  - ➤ **Objects**, for example a stick which is half immersed in water, **will appear bent at the surface**.

Step II Be the Teacher

This question is followed by three model answers.

One of these answers is a Grade A answer (above 80% correct), another a Grade C answer (around 50% correct). The third answer could be any grade (A to E).

Mark all three answers giving an appropriate grade with reasoning.

Question

Explain why objects in water appear closer to the surface than they actually are.

[4 marks]

Answer 1

When light passes into water it is slowed down and the rays of light are bent outwards. This is called refraction. The image you see of an object in the water is higher up as it forms as if the rays of light carried straight on and were not bent outwards.

| Mark | | Grade | |

Reasoning:...
....
....
....
....

Answer 2

refraction as light ray slowed down

image of fish

Mark		Grade	

Reasoning:..

....

....

Answer 3

Objects in water appear closer to the surface than they actually are because of refraction. This occurs because as the light travels through the water it is slowed down. It therefore takes longer to see the object so by the time you see it the object appears closer to the surface.

Mark		Grade	

Reasoning:..

....

....

....

Actual Mark and Grade for Question

Answer 1

When light passes into water it is slowed down and the rays of light are bent outwards. This is called refraction. The image you see of an object in the water is higher up as it forms as if the rays of light carried straight on and were not bent outwards.

Mark	4		Grade	A

Reasoning: A complete answer scoring all four marks scored for the following points:

- Refraction of light
- Slowing down of light ray in water
- Light rays bending further down to object
- Image formed higher up / image formed where light rays carry straight on

Answer 2

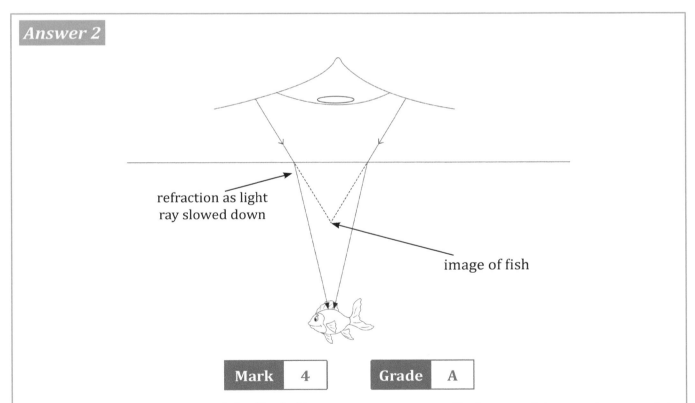

Mark	4		Grade	A

Reasoning: An accurate labelled diagram can score all the marking points and is often easier than putting into words. This diagram shows all four marking points so scores all four marks.

Step III Test Yourself

1. Complete this paragraph about refraction by putting in the correct word from the following list.

   | air   glass   denser   bent   closer   refracted   medium   normal |

   Refraction occurs when light travels from one transparent .... through another. The .... the medium the slower the light travels. Therefore light travels faster through .... than it does through .... If the light is slowed down passing through a transparent material then it is .... (bent) towards the .... line of material. Objects immersed in water appear .... to the surface due to refraction. An object half-immersed in water appears .... due to refraction. [8]

2. Complete the diagrams to show how each of these two light rays pass through the glass block. Identify the incident angle, refracted angle and emergent angle in each diagram.

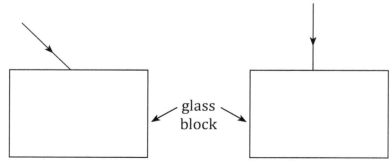

[6]

MODEL ANSWERS

1. Refraction occurs when light travels from one transparent **medium** [1] through another. The **denser** [1] the medium the slower the light travels. Therefore light travels faster through **air** [1] than it does through **glass**. [1] If the light is slowed down passing through a transparent material then it is **refracted** [1] (bent) towards the **normal** [1] line of material. Objects immersed in water appear **closer** [1] to the surface due to refraction. An object half-immersed in water appears **bent** [1] due to refraction.

2.

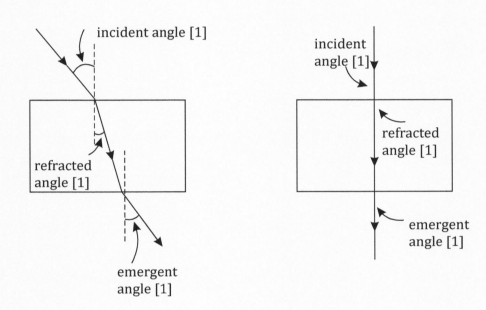

Total 14 marks

D. Dispersion of Light and Primary and Secondary Colours

Step I Key Knowledge

- **Dispersion** of the light is the **splitting of white light** into its **seven component colours (red, orange, yellow, green, blue, indigo and violet)**. This is called a spectrum of light.

- A **prism** (triangular glass block) **can cause dispersion of light** as it refracts (bends) each of the colours of white light by different angles. Red light bends the least and violet light bends the most. This is because the blue end of the spectrum has greater energy and is refracted more than the red end of the spectrum.

Common Errors

- A rainbow occurs when light is reflected off falling raindrops.

This is untrue as light passes through the raindrops and is dispersed. As each of the colours of white light are refracted (bent) by different angles.

- White light can be obtained by mixing **red, blue and green light**. We call these three colours **primary colours**.

Red + Blue + Green = White

- If we mix only two of these primary colours at a time, we obtain a **secondary colour**. The three secondary colours are:

Red + Blue = **Magenta**

Red + Green = **Yellow**

Blue + Green = **Cyan**

- The colour which an opaque object appears to have is the colour of the light that the object reflects into our eyes.

Common Errors

- A red tomato appears red as it absorbs the red light from the white light shining on it. This is false.

The tomato appears red as it absorbs the blue and green components of white light shining on it, and only reflects red light.

Step II Be the Teacher

This question is followed by three model answers.

One of these answers is a Grade A answer (above 80% correct), another a Grade C answer (around 50% correct). The third answer could be any grade (A to E).

Mark all three answers giving an appropriate grade with reasoning.

Question

A banana when it ripens changes from a green to a yellow colour.

Describe this colour change in terms of absorption and reflection of the primary colours of light (red, blue and green). [4 marks]

Answer 1

	Colours absorbed	Colours reflected
Green banana	Red and blue	Green
Yellow banana	Blue	Red and green

Mark [ ] **Grade** [ ]

Reasoning:..
....
....

Answer 2

A green banana absorbs all the green light that falls on it that is why it appears green in colour. The other primary colours like red and blue are reflected away.

A yellow banana absorbs all the yellow colour (red and green) and reflects away the blue part of the light.

Mark [ ] **Grade** [ ]

Reasoning:..
....
....

Answer 3

A green banana appears green as it only reflects green light. And absorbs the other colours (red and blue).

A yellow banana appears yellow as it absorbs yellow light as it is a mixture of red and green.

	Mark		Grade	

Reasoning:...

....

....

Actual Mark and Grade for Question

Answer 1

	Colours absorbed	Colours reflected
Green banana	Red and blue ✓	Green ✓
Yellow banana	Blue ✓	Red and green ✓

Mark	4	Grade	A

Reasoning: An excellent way to set out the answer. It is much clearer in table form what primary colours are being absorbed and reflected. It makes it easier for the examiner to mark, which also can be an advantage! All four marks are scored.

Answer 2

A green banana absorbs all the green light that falls on it that is why it appears greens in colour. The other primary colours like red and blue are reflected away.

A yellow banana absorbs all the yellow colour (red and green) and reflects away the blue part of the light.

Mark	0	Grade	E

Reasoning: The colour an object results from the colours that it reflects, not absorbs. The banana is green because it absorbs blue and red primary colours but reflects green primary colour. The candidate has this the wrong way around so scores no marks.

A green banana appears green as it only reflects green light. And absorbs the other colours (red and blue).

A yellow banana appears yellow as it absorbs yellow light as it is a mixture of red and green.

| Mark | 2 | | Grade | C |

Reasoning: Two marks are scored for the correct explanation of the colour of the green banana.

The yellow banana has the absorption and reflection of colours the wrong way around so scores no marks.

Step III Test Yourself

1. In the diagram below draw arrowed lines to link the correct primary colours that are needed to make the appropriate secondary colour.

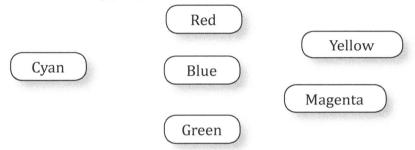

2. The glass prism causes the white light to undergo dispersion. Identify the colours (A to G) that are produced.

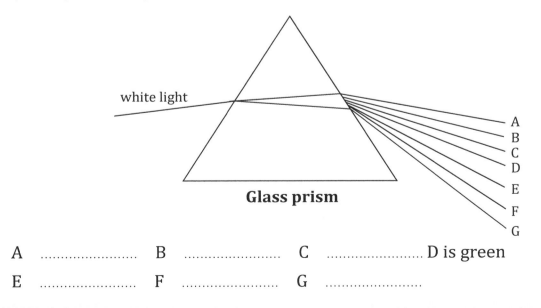

A .... B .... C .... D is green

E .... F .... G ....   [6]

3. A rock band wanted to wear red suits. They wished to appear invisible against a black backdrop at the start of the concert. State which of these four coloured filters over the white spotlight would make them appear black (before removing the filter and shining white light on the band, when their act started). Remember a particular colour filter only lets that coloured light through.

Blue filter   Red filter   Green filter   Yellow filter

Explain your choice of filters.

....

....

....

.... [4]

MODEL ANSWERS

1.

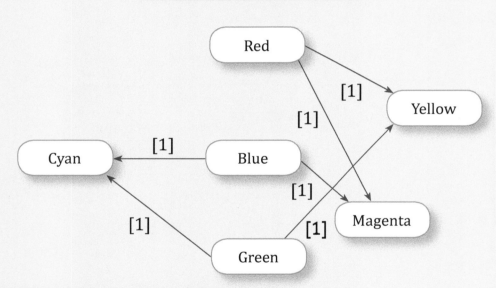

allow: arrows can point in either direction

2. A. red [1], B. orange [1], C. yellow [1], E. blue [1], F. indigo [1], G. violet [1]

3. Blue filter [1] (or green filter) would make them appear invisible as no red light passes through. [1]

Yellow filter (lets red and green light through) [1] and red filter would show up red suits as both let red light through. [1]

allow: blue filter appear black, green filter appear black, yellow filter appear red, red filter appear red

ignore: only two filters would appear black (unless state which two)

Examination Papers

Theme 1 Scientific Endeavour
Theme 2 Diversity
Theme 3 Models

PAPER 1

Multiple Choice

[Total 40 marks]   **(40 minutes)**

For each question there are four possible answers A, B, C and D. Choose the one you consider correct and record your answer in the bracket (   ).

Marks will not be deducted for wrong answers.

Calculators may be used.

1. Which of these statements about areas of scientific study is **incorrect**?
    A. Physics involves the study of different forms of energy.
    C. The measurement of electrical current is physics.
    D. The inter-relationship between plants and animals is biology.
    D. Chemistry involves the study of forces.

    [   ]

2. Identify the chemical that would have a hazard symbol of acutely toxic.
    A. Carbon dioxide   B. Chlorine   C. Common salt   D. Calcium carbonate

    [   ]

3. Which key gives the correct order for lighting a Bunsen burner?
    1. Strike a match   2. Switch on gas tap   3. Hold match above Bunsen chimney
    A. 1, 2 then 3   B. 1, 3 then 2   C. 2, 1 then 3   D. 2, 3 then 1

    [   ]

Questions 4 and 5

An experiment was carried out to collect the volume of gas given off in a chemical reaction every 10 seconds.

4. Name the apparatus that would be suitable to collect the gas given off in the experiment.
    A. Test tube   B. Conical flask   C. Gas syringe   D. Beaker

    [   ]

5. Which key identifies the dependent and independent variables in this experiment?

	Dependent variable	Independent variable
A	Volume of gas given off	Time taken
B	Amount of chemical left	Mass of gas given off
C	Time take	Volume of gas given off
D	Mass of gas given off	Amount of chemical left

[ ]

6. Identify which of these statements about salt water is/are correct.

1. Salt water is the solution   2. Water is the solute   3. Salt is the solvent

A. 1 only   B. 1 and 2   C. 1 and 3   D. 1, 2 and 3

[ ]

7. In the table below which key correctly identifies **all three** substances?

	Compound	Mixture	Element
A	Oil	Air	Steel
B	Wine	Beer	Alcohol
C	Paint	Rust	Iron
D	Common salt	Salt water	Oxygen

[ ]

8. Which of these would be a controlled variable in an experiment to decide which liquid heats up the quickest?

A. Stopping the clock at exactly the same point and time.

B. Using the same thermometer.

C. Starting the clock at exactly the same time.

D. Using the same volume of the different liquids.

[ ]

9. Select those attitudes that are useful during scientific inquiry.

1. Open-mindedness   2. Perseverance   3. Integrity

A. 1 and 2   B. 1 and 3   C. 2 and 3   D. 1, 2 and 3

[ ]

10.

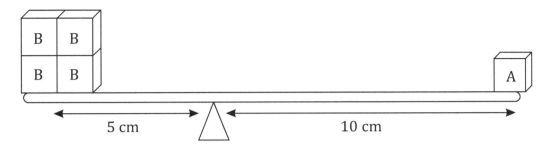

Which key correctly identifies the densities of Block A and Block B? You may assume the size of all the blocks are identical and the lever is balanced.

	Density of A	Density of B
A	0.25 g/cm³	1 g/cm³
B	4.0 g/cm³	1 g/cm³
C	4 g/cm³	2 g/cm³
D	2 g/cm³	4 g/cm³

[   ]

11. Identify the mixture that can be separated by adding water, stirring and then by filtration.

   A. Sand and grit   B. Sand and chalk   C. Sand and sugar   D. Sugar and salt

[   ]

12. The following chromatogram was obtained by a food scientist during an experiment to determine the different dyes used in the manufacture of sweet A and sweet B.

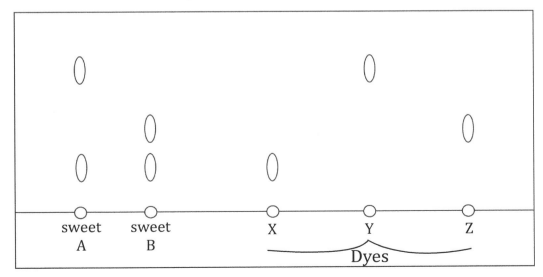

Which of these statements is **incorrect**?

A. Sweet A contains dyes X and Y.

B. Both sweets A and B contain two dyes.

C. Dye Z is present in both sweets A and B.

D. Sweet B contains dyes X and Z.

[   ]

13. Identify the change that would increase the rate of evaporation of a liquid.

A. Increasing the surface area of the liquid.

B. Lowering the temperature of the liquid.

C. Placing a lid over the liquid.

D. Dissolving a substance in the liquid.

[   ]

14. Which of these graphs best shows how the temperature of water in a beaker would change if it was heated by a Bunsen burner?

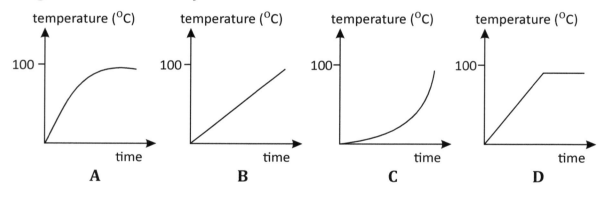

15. In which of these situations would it be wise to wear eye protection (**safety goggles**)?

A. Filtering a mixture of sandy water.

B. Evaporating a salt solution.

C. Setting up a paper chromatography experiment.

D. Separating iron filings from a mixture using a magnet.

[   ]

16. Identify the material that is classified **incorrectly**.

	Material	Classification
A	Nylon	Fibre
B	Glass	Ceramic
C	Zinc	Metal
D	Cotton	Plastic

[ ]

17. Which of these statements correctly describes the liquid water?
    1. Water has a definite shape.
    2. Water has a definite volume.
    3. Water has a definite melting point and boiling point.

    A. 1 and 2   B. 1 and 3   C. 2 and 3   D. 1, 2 and 3

[ ]

18. Identify which key correctly identifies both elements as metal and non-metal.

	Metal	Non-metal
A	Carbon	Nickel
B	Nickel	Sulfur
C	Carbon	Sulfur
D	Sulfur	Nickel

[ ]

19. Which statement correctly distinguishes a suspension from a solution?
    A. A suspension is a compound, a solution is a mixture.
    B. A suspension is transparent, a solution is opaque.
    C. A suspension can be separated by filtration, a solution by evaporation.
    D. A suspension is a solid dissolved in a liquid, a solution is a gas dissolved in a liquid.

[ ]

20. Desalination is the _____
    A. removal of undissolved solids.
    B. separation of liquids of different boiling points.
    C. removal of impurities in a mixture.
    D. removal of dissolved solids from sea water.

[ ]

21. Which key shows the correct classification of **both** living organisms?

	Plant Kingdom	Animal Kingdom
A	Algae	Shellfish
B	Bacteria	Spider
C	Grass	Fern
D	Toadstool	Bacteria

[   ]

22. Biodiversity is _____

   A. variety of life on earth.

   B. different types of animals in a family.

   C. different species of plants in a family.

   D. distinguishing characteristics of plants and animals.

[   ]

23. Select the animal that is a vertebrate.

   A. Insect   B. Snake   C. Crab   D. Scorpion

[   ]

24. Which of the statements about the Plant Kingdom is/are correct?

   1. All plants reproduce by asexual reproduction.

   2. Green plants photosynthesise 24 hours every day.

   3. All plants are producers.

   A. 1 and 2   B. 1 and 3   C. 2 and 3   D. 3 only

[   ]

25. Identify the statement that correctly distinguishes a spider from a fly.

   A. A spider lives indoors and a fly lives outdoors.

   B. A spider has 3 sections to its body while a fly has 2 body sections.

   C. A spider has 8 legs and insect 6 legs.

   D. A spider is warm-blooded but an insect is cold-blooded.

[   ]

26. Which of these is only found in plant cells?

   A. Cell membrane   B. Cell wall   C. Cytoplasm   D. Chromosomes

[   ]

27. Select the system responsible for providing energy to a living organism.

    A. Respiratory system

    B. Reproductive system

    C. Digestive system

    D. Nervous system

    [   ]

28. The fixed temperature at which all of a solid changes to a liquid is called its _____ .

    A. conduction point   B. boiling point   C. freezing point   D. melting point

    [   ]

29. Which key correctly identifies the changes of state associated with the named process?

	Named process	Changes of state
A	Evaporation	Solid to gas
B	Freezing	Solid to liquid
C	Sublimation	Liquid to gas
D	Condensation	Gas to liquid

    [   ]

30. Which of these would you expect to expand the most on heating?

    A. A block of copper metal

    B. Cold air

    C. Pure distilled water

    D. Mercury liquid

    [   ]

31. Identify those particles that are found in the nucleus of an atom.

            1. Proton   2. Electron   3. Neutron

    A. 1 and 2   B. 1 and 3   C. 2 and 3   D. 1, 2 and 3

    [   ]

32. Which atom has the correct number of sub-atomic particles?

	Number of electrons	Number of neutrons	Number of protons
A	6	6	7
B	7	6	7
C	7	8	7
D	8	7	7

[   ]

33. In the diagram the symbols $\triangle \lozenge \bigcirc$ represent atoms of different elements.

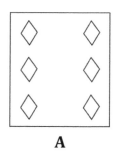 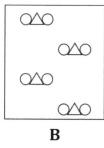 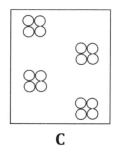 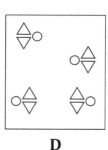

| A | B | C | D |

Which key represents a **molecule** of only **one** element?

[   ]

34. The chemical formula for copper sulfate is $CuSO_4$. Which key correctly identifies the number of atoms and elements?

	Number of atoms	Number of elements
A	3	6
B	6	3
C	7	4
D	7	3

[   ]

35. Which of these chemical formulae contains three atoms?

      1. SO_2 2. $CuCl_2$ 3. MgO

  A. 1 and 2   B. 1 and 3   C. 2 and 3   D. 1, 2 and 3

[   ]

36. Identify which is the luminous object?

  A. Cloud   B. Earth   C. Moon   D. Sun   [   ]

37. The diagram shows a ray of light reflected at a plane mirror.

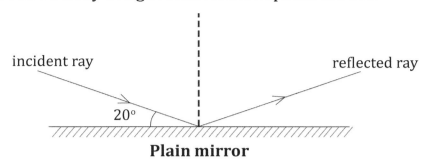

Plain mirror

Which of these angles of incidence and reflection are correct?

	Angle of incidence	Angle of reflection
A	20°	20°
B	20°	70°
C	70°	20°
D	70°	70°

[ ]

38. Which key correctly identifies what the word DROP would look when viewed in a plane mirror?

A. ꟼOЯꓷ   B. ꓷЯOꟼ   C. ꓷЯOꟼ   D. DROꟼ

[ ]

39. Select the key which correctly identifies the speed of light as it passes through a beaker of water.

	Incident ray from the air	Refracted ray in the water	Emergent ray from the water
A	Normal speed	Slows down	Speeds up
B	Normal speed	Speeds up	Slows down
C	Normal speed	Slows down	Slows down
D	Normal speed	No change in speed	No change in speed

[ ]

40. Identify which statement correctly explains why an object has a white appearance.

A. The object reflects red, blue and green light.

B. The object absorbs red light but reflects green and blue light.

C. The object absorbs red and blue light but reflects the green light.

D. The object absorbs red, blue and green light.

[ ]

[Total 60 marks] PAPER 2 **(1 Hour 15 minutes)**

Section A

[Total 30 marks] (35 minutes)

Answer all questions in the space provided.
The number of marks is given in brackets at the end of each question or part question.
Marks will not be deducted for wrong answers.
Calculators may be used.

1. Consider these eight different materials all beginning with 's'.

    Silver   Silk   Salt   Steel   Sulfur   Sodium   Sand   Sugar

    (a) Identify the three materials that have a high thermal conductivity.

    .... [2]

    (b) Identify the material that would be classed as a fibre.

    .... [1]

    (c) Identify the material that would be classed as a mixture as it is an alloy

    (mixture of metals). .... [1]

    (d) Identify the three materials that would be classed as compounds.

    .... [2]

2.

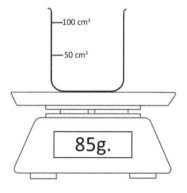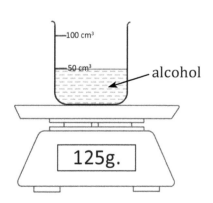

From the above diagrams deduce the density of alcohol.

....

....

....[3]

3. The diagram below shows the apparatus that is used for distillation.

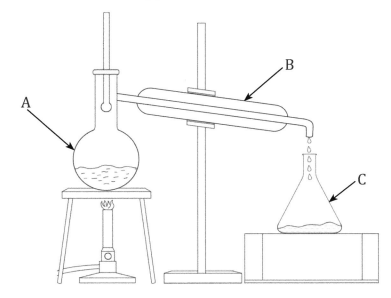

(a) Identify the three labelled pieces of apparatus.

A. ....   B. ....   C. ....   [3]

(b) Explain how the distillation apparatus works.

....

....

.... [3]

4. Immy and her friends were discussing the different parts of a cell.

> A thick rigid layer around the cell membrane.
>
> Immy

> Partially permeable layer around the cytoplasm.
>
> Oscar

> Jelly like substance that surrounds the nucleus.
>
> Unity

> Contains thread-like hereditary materials.
>
> Marianne

> Controls chemical reactions in the cell.
>
> Amanda

> Tiny discs containing a green substance that can absorb sunlight.
>
> James

(a) Name the friends that are describing parts of a cell that are **only** found in a plant cell.

.... [2]

(b) Name the friends that are describing the nucleus of the cell.

.... [2]

(c) Identify the friend that is describing the cell membrane.

.... [1]

5. Zunaida was making some revision notes about changes of state. However she accidentally spilled her drink over some of the notes which smudged some of the words. Can you replace the smudged words from the selection below.

compressed   boiling point   melts   volume   closely   gas   energy   vibrate

The particles in a solid are packed ✱ together and ✱ about fixed positions. On heating they gain ✱ and move further apart. When they can move freely the solid ✱ and becomes a liquid. Further heating moves the particles even further apart and the liquid changes to a ✱ The ✱ is the temperature when all particles have enough energy to become a gas. All gases can be ✱ and have no fixed shape or ✱ [8]

6. Complete this ray diagram to show how the ray of light is reflected off the four plane mirrors into the person's eye.

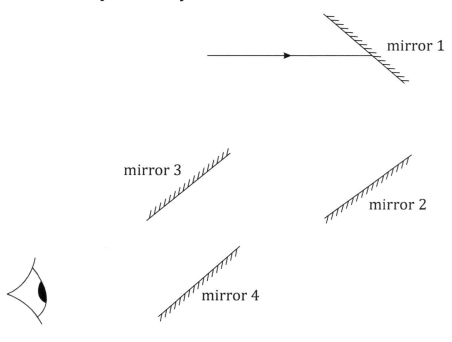

[2]

[Total 30 marks]   **(40 minutes)**

Answer all questions in the space provided.

The number of marks is given in brackets at the end of each question or part question.

Marks will not be deducted for wrong answers.

Calculators may be used.

1. A experiment was carried out to collect the gas given off in a chemical reaction. A diagram of the apparatus used is shown below.

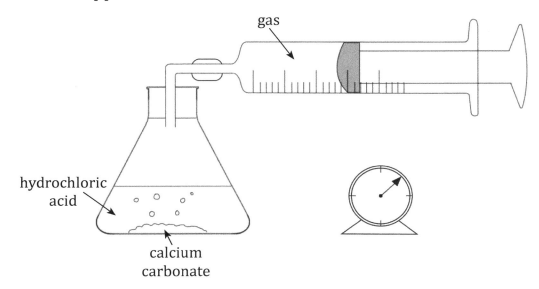

The volume of gas collected every half minute is shown in the table.

Time (minutes)	0.0	0.5	1.0	1.5	2.0	2.5	3.0	3.5	4.0
Volume (cm³)	0	45	75	90	95	99	100	100	100

(a) Name the piece of apparatus the gas is collected in.

.... [1]

(b) Identify these variables in the experiment.

    (i)   Independent variable .... [1]

    (ii) Dependent variable .... [1]

(c) (i) Plot a graph of volume of gas given off (y-axis) against time (x-axis).

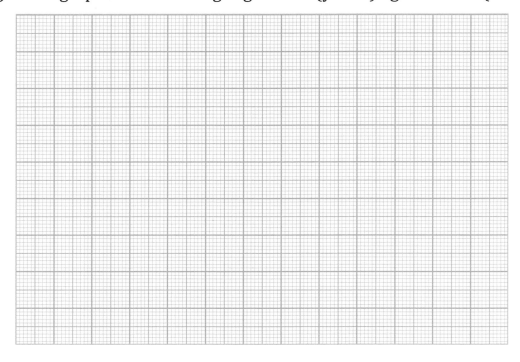

[6]

(ii) Use the shape of the graph to explain how the speed of the chemical reaction changes with time.

....

....[2]

(iii) State the time when the chemical reaction was complete. How is this shown on the graph?

....[2]

(d) The chemicals inside the conical flask were calcium carbonate ($CaCO_3$) and hydrochloric acid (HCl)

(i) Identify the three elements present in calcium carbonate.

....[2]

(ii) Identify the two elements present in hydrochloric acid.

....[2]

(iii) Complete the word equation for the chemical reaction that takes place.

.... + ...

⟶   calcium chloride + water + ... [3]

2. Construct a dichotomous key to identify these five vertebrate animals. [10]

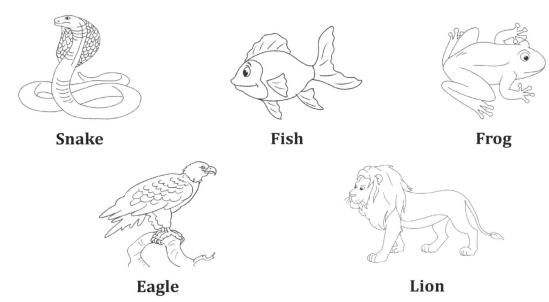

Snake   **Fish**   **Frog**

Eagle   **Lion**

Glossary

Atom	Smallest particle of an element that can take part in a chemical reaction.
Arthropod	Invertebrate animal with jointed legs such as insect, bee, butterfly.
Biodiversity	The total number of living plants and animals in a particular area.
Biology	The study of living organisms from the tiniest microscopic organisms to the largest whales.
Boiling point	Lowest temperature at which all of a liquid becomes a gas or vapour.
Cell	Tiny basic unit of living material. All living organisms are made up of one or more cells.
Cell membrane	Thin partially-permeable outer skin around the cytoplasm of the cell.
Cell wall	Thick, rigid outermost cellulose layer of a plant cell.
Chemical formula	This shows the number and type of atom present in the chemical substance.
Chemical reaction	Involves a rearrangement of atoms to form new molecules.
Chemical symbol	One or two letters to represent an atom of a particular element.
Chemistry	The study of molecular structures of matter and their interaction.
Chlorophyll	Pigment in plants which absorbs light energy from the sun to start the photosynthesis process.

Chloroplast	Structure (organelle) in the cytoplasm of the plant cell which contains chlorophyll.
Chromosomes	Tiny thread like coils of DNA found in the nucleus of a cell. They contain hereditary materials (genes).
Chromatography	Method of separating mixtures, especially coloured substances.
Compound	Substance formed when two or more different elements chemically combine together.
Condensation	Changing of a vapour (gas) into a liquid on cooling.
Conservation of Mass	During chemical and physical reactions no particles are lost or gained. The total mass of particles remains the same.
Controlled variable	A variable in an experiment that you do not change and which you keep the same, so that it is a fair test.
Corrosive	Describes chemicals like acids which eat away material.
Crystallisation	Method of separating mixtures by concentrating solutions with heating and then cooling the solution, so that crystals form.
Cytoplasm	Jelly like substance that lies between the nucleus and the cell wall. It is the protoplasm found outside of the nucleus.
Density	Mass per unit volume of a substance (units are g/cm^3, kg/m^3).
Dependent variable	A variable in an experiment that you measure. This variable is usually plotted on the y-axis of a line graph.
Desalination	Removal of salt from sea water to obtain fresh drinking water.
Dichotomous key	Diagram which classifies things by dividing them into two smaller groups each time.
Diffusion	Movement of particles from a region of higher concentration to a region of lower concentration.
Dispersion	Splitting of white light into its component colours to form a spectrum.
Distillation	Process by which a liquid is separated from a mixture, such as a solution.

Division of labour	Breakdown of the workload into smaller and more specific tasks to increase efficiency.
Ductile	Material which can be drawn into wire shape without breaking. Metals are usually ductile.
Eclipse	The total or partial blocking of sunlight when one celestial body (Earth or Moon) passes in between the Sun and the other celestial body.
Electrolysis	Chemical decomposition produced when electricity is passed through chemical solutions or molten compounds.
Electron	Negatively charged sub-atomic particle which is found in all atoms. Electrons orbit around the nucleus.
Elements	Substance which cannot be broken down into anything simpler by chemical means.
Evaporation	Process by which a liquid changes into a vapour (gas) at temperatures below its boiling point.
Extinction	Dying out of a particular animal or plant species so that none of that species are alive on Earth.
Filtrate	Clear liquid which passes through the filter paper.
Filtration	Process by which an insoluble solid is separated from a liquid.
Flammable	Describes a substance that can catch fire easily. Flammable substances have a hazard symbol on their container.
Genus	Closely related species of living organisms (plural genera).
Group	Vertical column of elements in the Periodic Table.
Homogenous	Describes solutions whose colour, density, appearance and other properties are the same in every part of the solution.
Hypothesis	Tentative explanation of a particular problem. It is one of the stages in scientific method.
Image	Picture of an object which a mirror, lens or optical instrument can produce.
Incident angle	Angle a light ray hits the reflective surface. It is measured to the normal line which is at 90° to the surface.

Independent variable	A variable in an experiment that you change. This variable is usually plotted on the x-axis on a line graph.
Inferring	Using observations and measurements to explain a happening.
Invertebrate	Describes an animal that does not have a backbone.
Kingdom	Main classification of living organisms. For example monera, protist, fungi, plant and animal kingdoms
Lateral inversion	Images from plane mirrors which are turned around from left to right.
Malleable	Material which can be flattened into thin sheets. Metals are often malleable.
Mass	Amount of matter an object contains (units are mg, g, kg).
Mass number	Total number of protons and neutrons in the nucleus of an atom.
Matter	Anything that has mass and occupies space.
Melting point	Lowest temperature at which all of a solid changes state and becomes a liquid.
Metals	Group of elements which are generally ductile, malleable, shiny and good conductors of heat and electricity.
Miscible	Describes liquids that dissolve in one another to form a single layer. An example is a water and alcohol mixture.
Mixture	Two or more substances that are not chemically combined together. Examples are air, alloys and crude oil.
Molecule	Two or more atoms chemically combined together.
Multicellular organisms	Plants or animals that are made up of more than one cell.
Neutron	Neutral sub-atomic particle found in the nucleus of atoms.
Non-metals	Group of elements which are generally dull in appearance and poor conductors of heat and electricity.
Neutron	Neutral sub-atomic particle found in the nucleus of atoms.

Nucleus	Small, heavy, central part of all atoms comprising of protons and neutrons.
Opaque	Surface that does not allow light to pass through.
Ore	Naturally occurring mineral from which metal is extracted.
Organ	Collection of tissues grouped together to perform a particular function such as the heart.
Parallax error	Error caused by reading the scale of an instrument at an angle. You should always read the scale of an instrument when looking vertically at it.
Partially- permeable membrane	Membrane which allows some molecules to pass through but not others. Also called a semi-permeable membrane.
Particulate theory	Theory that states all matter is made up of particles (atoms or molecules) which are moving in a random manner.
Period	Horizontal row of elements in the Periodic Table.
Periodic table	Systematic arrangement of all the different elements in the form of a chart.
Physics	The study of matter and energy including light, sound, radiation (heat), electricity, magnetism and motion.
Primary colour	Three colours red, blue and green which, when mixed together, produce. white light.
Proton	Positively charged sub-atomic particle found in the nucleus of all atoms.
Proton number	The number of protons (or electrons) in an atom of an element.
Real image	In optics, it applies to images that can be formed on a screen by light rays converging on it.
Reflected angle	Angle a light ray bounces off a reflective surface. It is measured to the normal line which is at 90° to the surface.
Reflection	Bouncing of light off a surface or object.
Refraction	Bending of light as it passes from one transparent material to another.

Residue	Solid that is trapped inside the filter paper during filtration.
Reverse osmosis	Process which uses high pressure to obtain fresh water from sea water (desalination). Also used in sewage purification.
Science	The systematic study of the world around us.
Scientific method	Step-by-step way used by scientists to analyse problems.
Secondary colour	Colour obtained when two primary colours are mixed together. The three secondary colours are magenta (red and blue), yellow (red and green) and cyan (blue and green).
Shadow	Area of darkness on a surface caused by an opaque object stopping light from reaching that surface.
Saturated solution	Solution which contains the greatest amount of solute that it can dissolve in a fixed volume of solvent, at a given temperature.
Solar evaporation	Using the heat of the Sun to naturally evaporate water. This is used in desalination of sea water.
Solubility	Amount of solid which will dissolve in 100 g of solvent, at a particular temperature.
Solute	Solid substance which dissolves in a solution. For example sugar in sugar solution.
Solution	Mixture of solute and solvent. For example sugar solution is a mixture of sugar and water.
Solvent	Liquid which dissolves the solute. For example water in sugar solution.
Species	Group of living organisms of the same kind. Members of the same species may breed with one another.
Spectrum	Colours formed when white light is split up by refraction through a glass prism.
State of matter	Solid, liquid and gas are the three states of matter.
Sublimation	Changing directly from a solid to a gas, without passing through the liquid state.

Suspension	Mixture formed when a fine-particle solid does not dissolve in a liquid (or gas).
System	Group of several organs working together to perform a particular function. For example the circulatory system or the reproductive system.
Technology	Use of scientific knowledge for practical purposes.
Tissue	Group of similar cells which perform a similar task or function.
Toxic	Describes a substance which is poisonous. Toxic substances have a hazard label on their container.
Unicellular organisms	Simple organisms (plant or animal) made up of only one cell.
Vacuole	Fluid filled space inside the cytoplasm of a cell. In plants cell vacuoles contain the cell sap.
Vapour	Gaseous state of a substance which is normally a liquid at room temperature and pressure.
Variable	Something that you change or control during experimentation. There are three main types of variable: dependent, independent and controlled.
Vernier	Scale attached to the main scale of an instrument so that the instrument can be read more accurately.
Vertebrate	Animals with backbones. Examples are fish, amphibian, reptiles, birds and mammals.
Virtual image	Applies to images that cannot be put onto a screen (like the image of a plane mirror)
Zero error	Reading an instrument gives when it is not reading anything and should be zero.

Answers

PAPER 1

Section A

1. **D.** The study of forces is Physics and not chemistry.

2. **B.** Chlorine gas is acutely toxic.

3. **B.** The correct order for lighting a Bunsen burner is to strike a match and then hold the match above the Bunsen chimney. Lastly you should then switch on the gas tap to ignite the Bunsen flame.

4. **C.** A gas syringe would be suitable to collect the gas given off in a chemical reaction.

5. **A.** The dependent variable is the volume of gas given off. The independent variable is the time taken.

6. **A** Salt water is the solution in which water is the solvent (dissolving liquid) and salt is the solute (solid that has dissolved).

7. **D** Common salt is a compound whose chemical name is sodium chloride ($NaCl$). Salt water is a mixture of water and the dissolved salt. Oxygen is an element.

   Option A: Oil, air and steel (alloy of iron and carbon) are all mixtures.

   Option B: Wine and beer are mixtures and alcohol is a compound (ethanol C_2H_5OH)

   Option C: Paint is a mixture, rust a compound (hydrated iron oxide $Fe_2O_3.H_2O$) and iron is an element.

8. **D.** Using the same volume of different liquids is a controlled variable in an experiment to decide which liquid heats up the quickest.

9. **D.** Open-mindedness, perseverance and integrity are all useful attitudes for scientific inquiry.

10. **C.** For the lever to balance the moments of the forces either side must be equal. $((4 \text{ g/cm}^3 \times 1) \times 10 \text{ cm}) = ((2 \text{ g/cm}^3 \times 4) \times 5 \text{ cm}) = 40 \text{ g/cm}^2$

11. **C.** Sand is insoluble in the water whereas the sugar dissolves. The mixture can therefore be separated by filtration.

Option A: Both sand and grit are insoluble in water and therefore cannot be separated by filtration.

Option B: Both sand and chalk are insoluble in water and therefore cannot be separated by filtration.

Option D: Both sugar and salt are soluble in water and therefore cannot be separated by filtration.

12. C. Dye Z is only present in sweet B and is not present in sweet A.

13. A. Increasing the surface area of a liquid would increase the rate of evaporation of the liquid.

    Option B: You would need to raise the temperature to increase rate of evaporation.

    Option C: In closed vessels with lids liquids cannot evaporate into the air.

    Option D: Dissolving substances in a liquid makes it more difficult for liquid particles to escape as the dissolved particles 'get in the way'. The rate of evaporation is therefore decreased.

14. A. The temperature rise of the water is quicker to start with, and then slows down. The temperature stays the same when it reaches 100 °C as this is the boiling point of water when all water changes into steam.

15. B. Evaporation involves heating so as a precaution eye protection should be worn. This is because the liquid may spit when it boils and bubbles.

16. D. Cotton is a natural fibre and not an artificial plastic material. Cotton is spun from the seeds of the cotton plant.

17. C. Water has a definite volume and a definite melting point (0 °C) and boiling point (100 °C).

    Options A, B and D: Water does not have a definite shape but takes on the shape of the container it is held in.

18. B. Nickel is a metal and sulfur is a non-metal.

    Option A: Carbon is a non-metal and nickel is a metal.

    Option C: Both carbon and sulfur are classified as non-metals.

    Option D: Sulfur is a non-metal and nickel is a metal.

19. C. A suspension can be separated by filtration as this removes the suspended solid particles present. Evaporation separates the dissolved solute (solid) by evaporating the solvent (liquid) part of the solution.

Option A: Both suspensions and solutions are mixtures.

Option B: A suspension is opaque and a solution transparent.

Option D: A suspension is a mixture of insoluble small particles in a liquid. A solution is a dissolved solid in a liquid.

20. D. Desalination is the removal of dissolved solids from sea water.

Option A: Filtration is the removal of undissolved solids.

Option B: Distillation is the separation of liquids of different boiling points.

Option C: There are many techniques to remove impurities from liquids like filtration, evaporation and distillation.

21. A. Algae is a simple member of the plant kingdom and a shellfish is an animal belonging to the crustacean group of invertebrates.

Option B: Bacteria are not part of the plant kingdom. They are a group of very simple organisms which make up their own separate kingdom.

Option C: Fern is a member of the plant kingdom. It is a seedless plant.

Option D: Toadstools are a member of the fungi kingdom. Bacteria have their own separate kingdom.

22. A   Biodiversity is variety of life on earth.

23. B   A snake is a vertebrate animal belonging to the reptile group.

Option A, C and D: Insects, crabs and scorpions are invertebrate animals as they do not contain a backbone.

24. D   All plants are producers and are found at the beginning of food chains.

Options A and B: Seedless plants (algae, ferns) reproduce by asexual reproduction but seed plant reproduce by sexual reproduction.

Options A and C: Green plants only photosynthesise when it's light, not 24 hours a day.

25. C   A spider has 8 legs (4 pairs) and an insect has 6 legs (3 pairs).

Option A: Spiders live indoors and outside in gardens, fields, woodland etc.

Option B: A spider has 2 sections to its body while a fly has 3 sections (head, thorax and abdomen).

Option D: Both spiders and insects are arthropods and are cold-blooded invertebrates.

26. B.   A cell wall is only found in plant cells.

   Options A, C and D: Cell membrane, cytoplasm and chromosomes are all found in both plant and animal cells.

27. A   The respiratory system provides energy for the living organism.

   Option B: The reproductive system produces new offspring.

   Option C: The digestive system helps to break down food into small soluble molecules.

   Option D: The nervous system carries electrical impulses through the living organism.

28. D.   The fixed temperature at which all of a solid changes to a liquid is called its melting point.

   Option B: The fixed temperature at which all of a liquid changes to a gas/vapour is called its boiling point.

   Option C: The fixed temperature at which all of a liquid changes to a solid is called its freezing point.

29. C.   Sublimation changes a liquid to a gas (or vice versa).

   Option A: Evaporation changes a liquid to a gas /vapour.

   Option B: Freezing changes a liquid to solid.

   Option D: Condensation changes a gas /vapour to a liquid.

30. B.   Cold air is a gas and would therefore expand the most.

   Options A, C and D: On heating solids expand the least, then liquids, and gases expand the most.

31. B.   Protons and neutrons are found in the nucleus of atoms.

   Options A, C and D: Electrons are always found orbiting around the nucleus, never inside the nucleus

32. C.   In an atom the number of protons (positive charge) must always equal the number of electrons (negative charge) as the atom has an overall neutral charge.

   Option B: The number of neutrons is never less than the number of protons/ electrons. It can be the same or slightly greater in number.

33. C.   Elements contain only one type of atom but a molecule of an element must have more than one of this atom present.

Option A: This is an element as it contains only one atom. However it is not a molecule (group of atoms)

Options B and D: These contain two types of atom and therefore cannot be elements.

34. B. Copper sulfate ($CuSO_4$) contains 3 elements and a total of 6 atoms (1 copper, 1 sulfur and 4 oxygen).

35. A. SO_2 contains 1 sulfur and 2 oxygen atoms. $CuCl_2$ contains 1 copper atom and two chlorine atoms. Both these molecules contain 3 atoms in total.

Options B, C and D: MgO contain 1 magnesium atom and 1 oxygen atom. A total of two atoms.

36. D. The Sun is a luminous object as it gives off light.

Options A, B and C: Clouds, Earth and Moon do not give off any natural light so are non-luminous objects. They can all reflect sunlight, for example moonlight.

37. D. The angle of incidence is measured to the normal line, so equals 70°. The incident angle is always equal to the angle of reflection (70°).

38. A Lateral inversion occurs so the image is back to front and each letter turned the other way around. This is only shown in key A.

39. A. Light travels slower when passing through a denser medium. The refracted ray therefore travels slower in the water. On leaving the water into the air the emergent ray would speed up back to its normal speed in the air.

40. A. An object has a white appearance as it reflects all the primary colours (red, blue and green).

Option B: An object would appear cyan (greenish–blue) if it reflected green and blue light.

Option C: An object would appear green if absorbs red and blue light but reflects the green light

Option D: An object which absorbs all the primary colours of red, blue and green would appear black.

Section A

1. (a) Silver, Steel, Sodium (all metals) [2],   (b) Silk [1],

    (c) Steel [1],   (d) Salt, Sand and Sugar [2]

2. Mass = 125 g – 85 g = 40 g, Volume = 50 cm³ [1]

    Density = Mass / Volume [1] $= 40 \text{ g} / 50 \text{ cm}^3 = 0.8 \text{ g} / \text{cm}^3$ [1]

3. (a) A = round-bottomed flask [1], B = condenser [1], C = conical flask [1]

    (b) Water is heated in the round-bottomed flask and evaporates. [1]
      The vapour passes through the condenser, which cools it down and
      condenses the vapour. [1]
      The liquefied vapour then trickles into the conical flask. [1]

4. (a) Immy and James [2], (b) Marianne and Amanda [2], (c) Oscar (1)

5. The particles in a solid are packed **closely** [1] together and **vibrate** [1] about fixed positions. On heating they gain **energy** [1] and move further apart. When they can move freely the solid **melts** [1] and becomes a liquid. Further heating moves the particles even further apart and the liquid changes to a **gas** [1]. The **boiling point** [1] is the temperature when all particles have enough energy to become a gas. All gases can be **compressed** [1] and have no fixed shape or **volume** [1].

6.

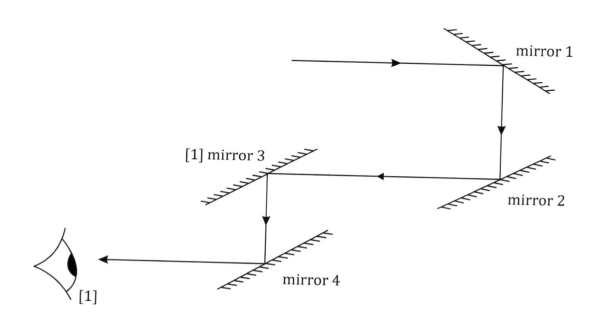

1. (a) gas syringe [1]

   (b) (i) Time [1], (ii) Volume [1]

   (c) (i) correct axes [2]   correct plotting [4]

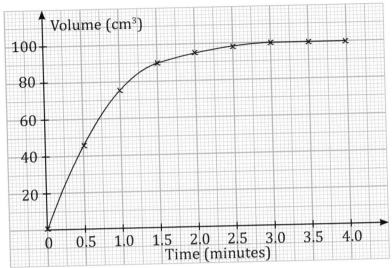

   (ii) The speed of the chemical reaction started quickly [1]
       and then slowed down. [1]

   (iii) The chemical reaction stopped after 3 minutes. [1]
       The flat line of the graph indicates that the reaction has stopped. [1]

   (d) (i) Calcium [1], Carbon and Oxygen [1]

   (ii) Hydrogen [1], Chlorine [1]

   (iii) Calcium carbonate [1] + Hydrochloric acid [1]

       → Calcium chloride + Water + Carbon dioxide [1]

2.

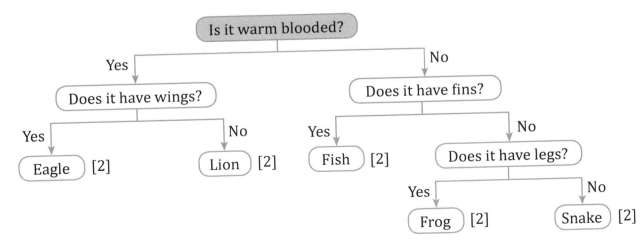